Early Music

by

Lucien Jenkins

Published by Naxos Books, an imprint of Naxos Rights International Ltd

© Naxos Books 2007

www.naxosbooks.com

Printed and bound in China by Leo Paper Group

Design and layout: Hannah Davies, Fruition – Creative Concepts

Website music compiled by Lucien Jenkins

Timeline: Hugh Griffith

Map illustrator: Arthur Ka Wai Jenkins

All photographs © Lebrecht Music & Arts Photo Library unless otherwise credited

ISBN: 978-1-84379-233-8

Contents

Website

Log onto **www.naxos.com/naxosbooks/discoverearly**
and hear over two hours of music, all referred to in the text.

To access the website you will need:

ISBN: 9781843792338
Password: Victoria

website Streamed at 64Kbps to provide good-quality sound.

website Easy links to view and purchase any of the original
CDs from which the extracts are taken.

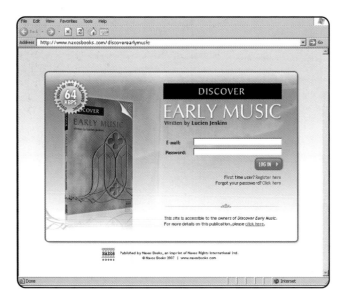

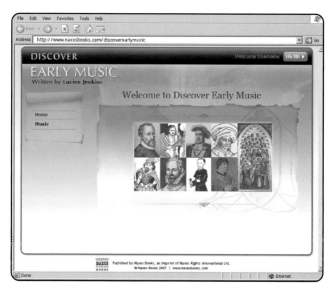

Early Music

by

Lucien Jenkins

Saint and angels playing music
Tempura on wood, c. 1335,
by Giotto di Bondone (c. 1266–1337) and workshop

I. What Were the Middle Ages?

In music, there are no sensible dates tied to composers' births or deaths to mark out the Middle Ages. For simplicity's sake, scholars largely adopt the period 500 AD to 1500 AD, this being roughly the time between the change of the western part of the Roman Empire into an interlocking series of kingdoms, and the Italian Renaissance and Reformation. The term 'Dark Ages' is also sometimes used, normally to describe the opening centuries of this period (say sixth to tenth), although some prefer the expression 'early Middle Ages'. Of course the men and women of the Middle Ages did not think of themselves as living in the middle of anything. In fact, they were more inclined to think they were living at the end of something. The Christian message of the time contained within it a strong belief that the return of Christ was imminent, that everything in the life of human beings was merely contingent, and that the essential life was the one that the returning Christ would institute. The early medieval Frankish chronicler Fredegar wrote sadly: 'The world is growing old. We live at the end of time.'

The Middle Ages inherited its legal code and much of its secular literature from the declining power of Rome.

Overwhelmed by economic and political developments that it could no longer direct, Rome had found that the several regions of its empire were acting with increasing independence. The various Burgundians, Franks, Lombards and others who had been problematic allies in the latter days of imperial power played a leading role, sometimes as semi-independent local rulers and sometimes, as in the case of Stilicho, Odoacer and Theodoric, as imperial agents. In the meantime, the challenge from outside Roman boundaries was transformed by the impact of the Huns in the fifth century. They were a substantial and powerful nation with a large empire and had no interest in adapting to the Roman diplomatic system. Indeed, throughout the Middle Ages the mobility of some nations created problems for other more settled societies. The Vikings, Saxons, Hungarians and Arabs were all on the move at different times. The last of these groups first came to European consciousness by seizing control of the Middle East in the seventh century. Three of the Christian patriarchates – Jerusalem, Alexandria and Antioch – were quickly overrun, leaving only Rome and Byzantium. By 718, most of what is now Spain and Portugal was in Muslim hands, and there were also Muslim forces in southern France. It was not until the late fifteenth century that the last Muslim stronghold in Spain fell to Christian armies, not many years after the Christian stronghold of Byzantium itself had finally fallen to a Muslim army, leaving the way clear for Islam to overrun south-eastern Europe, which it was to dominate for several centuries.

Despite these massive shifts of population and power, Roman laws, Roman language and Roman ways of thinking persisted throughout the Middle Ages and into the Renaissance. Indeed, the very fact that Rome was thought of as the natural home for the Church's 'capital' was in its way a tribute to the continued high standing of the city among western Christians. The Church enjoyed massive cultural, political and economic power and influence right across Europe throughout the Middle Ages. The virtual disappearance of the Roman administrative classes, together with the absence of any tradition of literacy in the new powers (Franks and others), meant that the business of law, diplomacy and government necessarily leaned heavily on the Church, which, based as it was around a series of books, held literacy in high esteem.

II. The Church and Music

The history of medieval music is inextricably bound up with the history of the Church. For a start, the first musical notation was developed in, for and by the Church. As a result, sacred music was, for much of the medieval period, pretty much the only repertoire to be written down, and this means our view of medieval music is heavily biased towards sacred vocal music. Music was an integral part of the liturgy (or church service), which means that every monastic church saw a daily round of musical performances, making the Church not only a major employer of musicians but also the key network of performance venues. This in turn influenced the style of the music itself: all those Romanesque and Gothic churches and cathedrals, with their high ceilings and consequently slow acoustic, did not encourage fast tempos.

Medieval sacred music ventured beyond the Church too: it moved out from the liturgy and the Eucharist into religious dramas, the indirect ancestor of opera. Music also moved into sacred vernacular song, the *lauda spirituali* or 'spiritual songs' such as the Spanish *cantigas de Santa Maria* and English carols – music which, though still setting texts that dealt with sacred topics, did not form part of a church service. *Cantiga* literally means 'song', but on the *Discover Early Music* website you can hear a *cantiga* given an instrumental performance (website 6), in contrast to the vocal account of the carol just before it (website 5).

Despite this, the Church treated music warily. It is true that most authorities favoured its use: the thirteenth-century philosopher and theologian Thomas Aquinas recognised the influence it exercised on a worshipper's mind. But some were anxious that music could become worldly and regarded it with suspicion: Pope John XXII wrote in the fourteenth century that he opposed the use of polyphony (music using two or more melody lines simultaneously) because having more than one tune playing at the same time prevented people from understanding the text that was being sung.

Plainchant

Early medieval Europe became divided into a series of kingdoms: Franks, Goths, Lombards and Saxons, with the Church the only remaining unifying force (and thus in the West, the heir of the Roman Empire). Political divisions implied cultural divisions, and just as there were regional styles in the visual arts, so there were different repertoires of melodies for singing sacred texts. However, despite these differences the assumption that the Roman Empire had not altogether gone away never quite faded, and there continued to be a high level of respect for the Roman inheritance and indeed for the continuing Roman Empire that lay in the eastern Mediterranean, with its capital at Byzantium. By the end of the eighth century, the most powerful political and military force in western Europe was the Franks. Inheriting a sizeable kingdom from his father, who had seized power, Charlemagne (which translates as 'Charles the Great') extended the kingdom still further, conquering several neighbours. He also answered an appeal for help from Pope Desiderius, who was embroiled in a struggle with the Lombards. Crowned the first new emperor of the West on Christmas Day, 800, Charlemagne's Roman ambitions meant that he took the politically driven decision to standardise the western liturgy around Roman lines. This led to plainchant repertory being written down for the first time.

No musical sound is more characteristic of the Middle Ages than plainchant. Some of these chant melodies undoubtedly came into western Europe from the eastern Mediterranean and are therefore very ancient, but because chant is largely anonymous it is very difficult to identify exactly which the very ancient ones are. Dating back to the early Church, these melodies preserve elements of pre-Christian musical practice. Similarly, iconographers have made a clear and convincing link between Christian practice in the visual arts and pre-Christian models.

The Church knew perfectly well that music was a useful tool for the conversion and retention of worshippers. Nevertheless, although Christians were allowed to use a lyre to accompany themselves when singing hymns and psalms at home, instrumental music was largely excluded from the Church. This meant that it was dominated by unaccompanied plainchant. Chant is essentially heightened speech. In that sense it is a close relation of recitative, that curiously declamatory form of singing in eighteenth-century opera that

St Ambrose, a bishop of Milan, was introduced to St Augustine of Hippo by the young man's mother St Monica (Ambrose was her confessor), and converted him to Christianity.

'Some claim that I have ensnared the people by the melodies of my hymns. I do not deny it.'

helps keep the plot moving along between arias. It also belongs to the same family as rap and hip-hop. Mozart, Eminem and St Ambrose may seem like odd companions, but they have in common the fact that they all prioritise words over melodies. If you can't follow the recitative sections, you'll have no idea what's happening on Figaro's wedding day, what trailer-park poor whites are angry about, or what's so big about the Christian message.

For centuries plainchant melodies were passed down orally and retained in singers' memories. Choirs rarely wrote them down because they had no call to: change did not happen fast in musical practice, repertoire development or choir membership. Thus there was far less need for notation then than today, when things alter so much more rapidly. In the early medieval Church there was a range of different chant styles: on the website you can hear an example of Ambrosian chant (website 1), a repertoire associated with Milan, in northern Italy, and taking its name from St Ambrose, a fourth-century bishop of Milan. Medieval melodies were first written down at the end of the eighth century as part of Charlemagne's political policy to press for greater centralisation and standardisation.

The result of this move towards uniformity is generally known as 'Gregorian chant' (website 2). It was probably a hybrid, combining late-eighth-century liturgical practice in Rome and the Roman world with practices that were better known in Charlemagne's Frankish empire.

It was first called 'Gregorian' in the mid-ninth century, and there can be little doubt that roping Pope Gregory the Great into the business was intended to lend political authority to the new music. 'Gregory I' was a good name on which to hang the revised chant: it is like insisting that (say) Churchill, Gandhi or Nelson Mandela lies behind some political reform that you want to propose. The expression 'Gregorian chant' is sometimes used with regard to any monophonic medieval song with a Latin text, i.e. music consisting of a single, unaccompanied melodic line. But these days, music historians are more likely to use it to mean specifically the music of the Mass (introits, graduals, offertories and so on) and the office chants, following the Carolingian drive for uniformity. Other medieval songs (such as sequences, tropes and hymns) may be chant, but they aren't Gregorian chant.

As already noted, not all sacred music was written for the Mass. One example comes from Hildegard of Bingen (1098–1179), who was not only a composer but also a mystic and a religious writer, a painter and a nun; she even wrote a medical treatise. She recorded her visions in *Scivias* (best translated as 'Know [the ways of the Lord]'). We need to bear in mind that she was a composer who never attended a concert, and a dramatist who never went to a theatre. In that, of course, she was far from unusual in the Middle Ages. But because she lived a reclusive life, there is every chance that she never attended any kind of public secular performance at all, musical or otherwise. Dramatists were largely cut off from the greatest figures in European theatre, knowing no Greek tragedy: they would have known Rome's Seneca rather than Athens's Sophocles. There was very little by way of theatre as we understand it today, and of course there were no public concerts until the latter part of the seventeenth century. What Hildegard *did* hear was her

Hildegard of Bingen (1098–1179)
Her composition is inspired by the Holy Spirit around
her head; illustration from The Wiesbaden Codex

own nuns singing. Her knowledge of drama stemmed from the Mass, and for her the main theatre was the Church itself. Like the better-known *Ludus Danielis* or 'Play of Daniel', Hildegard's *Ordo virtutum* `website 3` (the title would be translated as 'Play of Virtues') is a kind of medieval chamber opera, and although it was not used in a church service and so did not have a liturgical context, we need to remember that the liturgy is the key to our understanding of the author's sense of drama. Her *Ordo* takes one of those sets of sculptures of virtues that can be found on the west front of Romanesque cathedrals, and sets them arguing with the Devil in a drama that may have been inspired by the story of Sigewize – a fellow countrywoman of the composer who was apparently besieged by a demon. The music is essentially a series of songs with a single melody.

Sacred song

Perhaps surprisingly, we are not entirely sure what medieval carols were for, but we do know that they were not specifically associated with Christmas. They were simply English songs (sometimes in English itself and sometimes Latin) consisting of a sequence of verses and choruses, the equivalent of the continental *lauda spirituale* and *rondeau*. The name itself derives from the French *carole*, which simply means a dance song. The link between singing and dancing is cemented into English by the word 'stanza': meaning a verse, it comes from the Italian word for standing still, confirming that in dance songs everyone sang the stanzas while standing still and then sang the chorus while dancing round in a circle.

So it may be best to think of religious carols as songs that do involve movement, but with a procession taking the place of the dance.

There are surviving examples of both monophonic (one melodic line) and polyphonic (more than one melodic line) carols, a combination that is sometimes used to back up the evidence that there were both courtly and popular carols. We also have both sacred and secular texts, but we probably ought to resist classifying them separately, given that their original singers are unlikely to have acknowledged any such division. It is quite easy to see that some songs of serious sacred intent could have been given a place in a sacred setting, while in a secular setting a procession could take place in which both songs to the Blessed Virgin and more straightforward seasonal songs such as *Gaudete Christus est natus* (website 5) might have been performed.

The Crusades caused a major upheaval in medieval Europe. They might be best understood as another outbreak of those huge migrations of peoples that had characterised the early Middle Ages, and which had strained the late Roman Empire to breaking point. Indeed, when Anna Comnena, a Byzantine princess, watched the arrival of the first Crusaders, she described them as the barbarians on the march again.

Given the disastrous consequences for Byzantium and the entire Christian community in the Middle East, it is hard to disagree with Comnena's analysis. But the Crusaders' own name for themselves was 'pilgrims'. They saw themselves as going to pray in the Holy Places, and to recapture them from the Muslim armies that had seized the area centuries before. Pilgrimages were more than the kind of medieval tourism that they are sometimes seen as today; they were a network of communications and cultural contacts that ran the length and breadth of Christendom, a kind of religious 'single market'. Chaucer himself wrote that going on pilgrimages was just something that came over people in the spring, a kind of natural force, the same as the force that drove leaves to grow. Pilgrims went to Canterbury, Montserrat, Santiago di Compostela, Rome, Jerusalem and many other centres where saints were reputed to be buried (the *Cantiga* at website 6 is specifically associated with the Black Madonna of Montserrat).

Anna Comnena was one of the most noted of Byzantine historians. She was born on 1 December 1083, the eldest child of the emperor whose life she was to chronicle. She had originally expected to become empress, and at one point, disappointed in this assumption, staged a rebellion. Not surprisingly she hated the enemies of Byzantium, so she should be assumed to be ill-balanced whenever writing about Armenians, Muslims and Crusaders. Her nomenclature can be confusing: for her, the Byzantines are 'the Romans', while the crusaders are variously 'Franks', 'Barbarians' and 'Celts':

'The stream of Time, irresistible, ever moving, carries off and bears away all things that come to birth and plunges them into utter darkness, both deeds of no account and deeds which are mighty and worthy of commemoration; as the playwright says, it "brings to light that which was unseen and shrouds from us that which was manifest". Nevertheless, the science of History is a great bulwark against this stream of Time; in a way it checks this irresistible flood, it holds in a tight grasp whatever it can seize floating on the surface and will not allow it to slip away into the depths of Oblivion.

I, Anna, daughter of the Emperor Alexius and the Empress Irene, born and bred in the Purple, not without some acquaintance with literature – having devoted the most earnest study to the Greek language, in fact, and being not unpractised in Rhetoric and having read thoroughly the treatises of Aristotle and the dialogues of Plato, and having fortified my mind with the Quadrivium of sciences (these things must be divulged, and it is not self-advertisement to recall what Nature and my own zeal for knowledge have given me, nor what God has apportioned to me from above and what has been contributed by Opportunity); I, having realised the effects wrought by Time, desire now by means of my writings to give an account of my father's deeds, which do not deserve to be consigned to Forgetfulness or to be swept away on the flood of time into an ocean of Non-Remembrance; I wish to recall everything, the achievements before his elevation to the throne and his actions in the service of others before his coronation.'

An anonymous eyewitness reports on the chaos and carnage of the First Crusade:

'Then the amir who held David's Tower surrendered to the count, and opened for him the gate where the pilgrims used to pay their taxes, so our men entered the city, chasing the Saracens and killing them up to Solomon's Temple, where they took refuge and fought hard against our men for the whole day, so that all the temple was streaming with their blood. At last, when the pagans were defeated, our men took many prisoners, both men and women, in the temple. They killed whom they chose, and whom they chose they saved alive. On the roof of the Temple of Solomon were crowded great numbers of pagans of both sexes, to whom Tancred and Gaston of Bearn gave their banners.

After this our men rushed round the whole city seizing gold and silver, horses and mules, and houses full of all sorts of goods, and they all came rejoicing and weeping from excess of gladness to worship at the Sepulchre of our Saviour Jesus, and there they fulfilled their vows to him. Next morning they went cautiously up on to the Temple roof and attacked the Saracens, both men and women, cutting off their heads with drawn swords. Some of the Saracens threw themselves down headlong from the Temple.'

III. Secular Music

We know disappointingly little about secular music in the
Middle Ages. The community of performers and composers
that included troubadours, minstrels and the performers of
epic poetry, the semi-legendary bards or scops, is not well
represented by the surviving written and notated evidence.
We do possess the texts of poetry such as the Old English (or
Anglo-Saxon) *Beowulf* and the Anglo-Norman French
Chanson de Roland ('Song of Roland'). We even know that an
earlier version of the Roland story than the one that has
survived was used to entertain and inspire the Norman army
immediately before the Battle of Hastings in 1066. The Old
English poem *Widsith* tells of the wanderings of a scop,
singing the tales of dead kings and heroes across the Saxon
world. Since only tiny fragments of the music to these poems
survive, we have no more to go on than descriptions of
performances (solo voices accompanied by a single
instrument such as a harp). Consequently, we know less about
this kind of music than we do about the songs of ancient
Babylon and Delphi.

Songs performed by goliards (a type of jester) were written
in Latin and thus the authors – and perhaps composers – were

by definition educated and, again by definition, part of the Church. The subject matter invariably concerns drinking, gambling or gluttony – in effect this was light entertainment for literary people. The name goliard itself may owe something to the Latin word for gluttony, *gula*; although the existence of references to an imaginary 'Bishop Golias' as supposed author of the disparate works suggests that the word could derive from Goliath of Gath, taken as a symbol of wickedness, an opponent of the biblical hero David. (David was of course a king and poet–composer himself, and traditionally accepted as the author of the Old Testament Book of Psalms.) Perhaps because of its link to the Church, a reasonable amount of goliardic material has survived, whereas the minstrels and *jongleurs* (from which English derives the work 'juggler', indicating that they were all-round entertainers) have left us nothing to go on, possibly because they were themselves illiterate.

A thirteenth-century manuscript, the *Carmina Burana,* or Burana Codex, was found in the Benediktbeuren monastery in Bavaria. It contains satirical songs full of worldly-wise advice and parodies (in the modern sense) of sacred songs, and these satires, plus the illustrations and the presence of Christian prayers and a Passion play, indicate that this manuscript includes material composed and written out by members of the Church. Most of the songs in the manuscript, however, have no music. For those that do, the neumes (medieval written signs, of which more later) that notate the tunes give little guidance for performers, who therefore need to take time to consider their interpretation of such an open document. On the website is *Exiit diluculo* (website 7), which tells of a dawn seduction in the countryside.

Today, most people have heard of the *Carmina Burana* or 'Songs of Beuren' (after Benediktbeuren) through Carl Orff's twentieth-century setting of some of them. But they were songs with their own music long before Orff encountered them. The manuscript, which dates from around 1230, is an anthology of work by several composers from the early decades of the thirteenth century. Although the manuscript itself is German, many of the songs whose authors are known are from France. Largely written in medieval Latin (there are a few in German and one that mingles Latin, French and Occitan), the songs often deal with corruption and church politics, again suggesting that they were written by clerics. It may sound strange to a post-Reformation world that clerics spent their time composing this kind of material but we have to remember that our own word for 'clerk' is descended from the same source as our word 'cleric'. Medieval clerics might have been priests in little more than name, filling posts that in a modern age are assigned to university dons, clerical workers and civil servants. The Church offered both a career path for those in search of education and social advancement, and a refuge from a few of the economic and social problems of the age: clerics were protected from secular law, for example.

Troubadours

Troubadours are among the best-known medieval performers, again because a reasonable amount of their material has survived. Unlike goliards, who came from a clerical world, troubadours were secular and had close links to the land-owning classes – indeed, some were themselves knights or

The testimony of one young woman named Grazide to the Inquisition during its investigations into heresy in southern France makes for disturbing reading:

'Seven years ago, or thereabouts, in summer, the priest Pierre Clergue came to my mother's house while she was out harvesting, and was very pressing: "Allow me," he said, "to know you carnally."

And I said: "All right."

At that time, I was a virgin. I think I was fourteen or fifteen years old. He deflowered me in the barn in which we kept the straw. But it wasn't a rape at all. After that, he continued to know me carnally until the following January. It always took place in my mother's ostal; she knew about it and was consenting. It happened chiefly during the day.

After that, in January, the priest gave me as wife to my late husband Pierre Lizier and after he had thus given me to this man, the priest continued to know me carnally, frequently, during the remaining four years of my husband's life. And my husband knew about it, and was consenting. Sometimes he would ask me: "Has the priest done it with you?"

And I would answer: "Yes."

And my husband would say: "As far as the priest is concerned, all right! But don't you go having other men."

But the priest never permitted himself to know me carnally when my husband was at home. We only did it when he was out.'

aristocrats, and one of the most notable was Duke William IX of Aquitaine. From the late eleventh to the thirteenth centuries, troubadours wrote lyric poetry, of which about 300 songs have survived.

The language in which they wrote was Occitan (though it is often referred to as Provençal), the language of the southern half of France and a relative of Old French, but quite distinct from it and by no means simply a dialect. The troubadours' subject matter included what modern scholars call 'courtly love', an elevated, semi-devotional relationship with women which some have linked to the cult of the Virgin Mary. Others have pointed to the absence of many lords on Crusades in this period and suggested that their wives occupied their role and thus took on a socially challenging position, admired as women, respected as rulers. Either or both of these theories may have contributed to the rise of this cult of unconsummated passion, which one of their number, the twelfth-century Jaufré Rudel, called 'amor de lonh' or 'love from afar'.

We know that Rudel himself lived in the mid-twelfth century, but other than a legend which has grown up from a contemporary poem – that he took part in the Second Crusade in 1147– little information about him exists. According to this legend, he became ill at sea, was taken ashore at Tripoli and died there. Part of Rudel's biography, or *vida*, is to be found in a readily available *Introduction to Old Occitan* by William Paden (Modern Language Association, 1998), and there has even been an opera based on his life by the modern Finnish composer Kaija Saariaho called (what else!) *L'amour de loin*.

Another important figure is Guiraut Riquier (c. 1230–

c. 1300), often referred to as 'the last of the troubadours'. His lifetime encompassed the wars that largely destroyed the Occitan aristocratic society which had supported his kind. The age of the troubadour came to an unhappy end amid a war waged against the southerners by Pope Innocent III and the northern French: the Albigensian Crusade.

This Crusade was launched in 1208 to destroy a heresy that was endemic in the area. The Albigensians took their name from the southern town of Albi, and their beliefs were Cathar, which meant that everything of the spirit was believed to be good and everything of the flesh to be bad. There was a priesthood of 'perfect', ascetic men who lived in a state of poverty that contrasted with the often wealthy and corrupt lifestyle of the Roman Catholic hierarchy. All this may sound just like the teachings of mainstream medieval Christianity, but that apparent similarity helps to explain its ready acceptance in the area, where it grew to become the dominant religion: the local people felt that in Catharism they were simply being offered 'real' Christianity. Theologically, the sect departed from orthodoxy by believing that souls were trapped in human bodies and that death was a release. All this formed part of a rejection of the Christian (and Jewish) understanding of creation: that it is God's work and that it is intended to be good, even if it (people included) sometimes falls short of that ideal, and even if the divine plan isn't understood. Catharism saw the world and physical life as inherently evil and ruled by a wicked God, quite unlike the entirely separate and different God of the spirit. This downgrading of physical life and this world meant that the distinction between marriage and adultery, for instance, seemed of less importance than it did in Roman Catholicism.

The Albigensian Crusade destroyed an entire social order and with it the native poetic and musical life that had depended on that order. As the troubadours were closely linked to the social structures of southern France, the defeat of the southern French knights in the Albigensian Crusade was a major blow to their way of life. Guiraut Riquier knew that he was at the end of his own tradition. One of his lyrics declares that song should be joyful, but he was oppressed by sorrow: he had, he sang, come into the world too late. His music is represented here by a hymn, *Humils forfaitz* `website 8`, which is not in praise of his lady but of 'Our Lady', the Virgin Mary. The international respect afforded to troubadours saved Riquier's life, for we know that after about 1260 he lived in Spain under the patronage of Alfonso X, a king known as 'el Sabio' ('the wise').

Such was the success of the troubadours that all the countries surrounding the Occitan-speaking south of France were keen to be visited by them, and under their influence developed troubadour traditions of their own. Northern France was soon home to poet–composers in the same mould called *trouvères*. German *Minnesinger* followed, and there were also Catalan and Italian troubadours. Modern ideas about national and cultural borders meant little at this time, and troubadours could travel freely through what we now call Spain, France, Germany and Italy and be received with respect. The great Italian poets Dante and Petrarch both adored the work of the troubadours, and Dante referred to one of them, Arnaut Daniel, as 'il miglior fabbro' ('the better craftsman'). In the early twentieth century, when T.S. Eliot wished to pay tribute to Ezra Pound, he picked up Dante's expression and used it as a dedication on the title page of *The Waste Land*.

When listening to the troubadour song by Riquier, remind yourself that the performances are based on the same surviving notation as plainsong. This means that we know the pitches but not the note values, so we know how high or low to sing a note, but not for how long. Editors of such music therefore have to study the natural speech rhythms of the text to work out appropriate rhythms.

IV. Notation

When medieval music was written down, symbols called neumes were used, as mentioned earlier. These are like modern notation in that they indicate pitches, but only relative to one another: you knew that from one note to the next you had to move up, stay where you were or move down, but where you started depended on where your voice was comfortable.

Take the example of Hildegard of Bingen. Two manuscripts survive of her *Symphonia armonie celestum revelationum*, or 'Symphony of the harmony of celestial revelations'. One was a copy made in her lifetime and in her own abbey, probably in around 1175; it is incomplete. Another manuscript, which *is* complete, was again compiled at her convent, but this time after her death. The music is written out, using neumes, as a single melodic line in free rhythm. So pitch is indicated but it is relative; there is nothing that we would call a clef or key signature, so the singers would choose the pitch of the opening note according to their own range and proceed from there. There is, of course, no metronome mark since we would have to wait another seven centuries for the invention of metronomes; modern performers, therefore, do not know how fast to take the piece. They do not know whether to pause between lines; neither do they know whether the music should be sung as a single-line solo song or whether other parts should be added. If other parts are added, should they be voices or instruments? Should there be a drone, or pedal note? Should there be added an additional part or parts moving in parallel motion, forming harmonies at the fourth, fifth or octave? We simply do not know.

Whatever their parentage, neumes appeared in western Europe in the ninth century and varied in appearance from region to region. Once again, what you learn from studying one manuscript will turn out to be misleading in another, since what appear to be the same symbols possess quite different meanings. As a result, music from a single source of uncertain provenance is largely impossible to transcribe and interpret with any certainty. It is a bit like code-breaking: less than a bare minimum of data to work with and you cannot be certain that you have interpreted it correctly.

The much later Gothic neumes (using 'square notation') are arranged on a recognisable stave or system of horizontal lines clarifying the pitch relationships within the totality of a piece. The number and significance of lines on the stave varied. In *Musica Enchiriadis*, dated to AD 860 or 900, the lines were set at the interval of a second, which meant that notes were all written on lines. In the work of Guido of Arezzo (c. 991/92–after 1033), dating from around about 1030, the lines were a third apart, allowing notes to be written between lines as well as on them. Guido also recommended colouring a chosen line and allotting to it a specified pitch. He suggested a red F, with a yellow C as an

Guido of Arezzo (c. 991/92–after 1033)

alternative. He also proposed that a letter be written at the front of at least one of the lines to denote pitch. This is the origin of the modern clef system.

The move to a standardised five-line stave probably reflected the wider range demanded of each voice in polyphonic music. Initially, higher voices, singing the organal line (a line added to decorate plainchant; we shall come to organum on page 42), had a five-line stave while the lower part (with the plainchant) remained on a four-line stave, though even this varied according to the demands of the parts being set out. Indeed, staves did not settle down into predictable sets of five lines until the Baroque, as until then scribes would add an exra line as and when circumstances seemed to demand one.

Finally, it is worth bearing in mind that throughout this period, performers – even when they were singing from printed music on a five-line stave of a kind that modern musicians would broadly recognise – were following notation that had no barlines and looked very different from modern notation. Today some specialists have revived this practice and found that it frees up the music and enables them to understand better the underlying 'rhetoric' of the rhythm or the drive of the speech rhythms.

V. Instruments

The next investigation is what this music was actually played on. Thanks to illustrations, sculptures and documents that name and describe them, we know a good deal about the range of instruments that existed in the Middle Ages.

We know that there were organs and bells in churches. We know, too, that there was a general understanding that some instruments were loud and some quiet – 'haut' and 'bas' in French – and that these were grouped accordingly, often as outdoor and indoor instruments. Outdoor instruments were to be found in what the English called 'waits' and the Italians 'piffari': ensembles of civic musicians that developed in towns and cities across much of Europe. Shawms (a kind of loud oboe), slide trumpets and sackbuts (early trombones) were much favoured in an ensemble that occupied the role filled in twentieth-century Britain by the brass band; like a band, this ensemble could be hired to play at a range of events, offering dance music, attending town functions, processions or even supporting a cathedral's choral music on special occasions. Alonso Mudarra (whose *Tiento* website 31 you can hear) persuaded those in power at Seville Cathedral, where he worked, to hire two shawm players for the Corpus Christi festival – an annual celebration instituted by Pope Urban IV in around 1263, originally as a procession but increasingly the focus of music and drama. You can hear some of these wind instruments on three tracks containing arrangements by the Flemish Renaissance musician Tylman Susato (website 19-21) (c. 1510/15–1570 or later), a successful trumpeter, publisher, composer and arranger from Antwerp.

There were also flutes, recorders, various drums, and plucked and bowed instruments. The visual evidence means that we know a good deal about the appearance of these instruments. Unfortunately, we know a great deal less about the specific music they played and the sound they made. Unlike all later periods in music history, there is no surviving piece of music from the Middle Ages that actually specifies a particular instrument. Nor are we sure in what combinations instruments were played. When modern players first attempted to perform medieval music, the fashion was for instrumental ensembles that looked a bit like folk groups or ceilidh bands. More recently, the tendency has been for just two or three players per work, and even solo performances. What kind of evidence do they have to go on in making this decision?

Despite the impression given by the soundtracks of costume dramas on film and television, the medieval audience thought on a modest scale. We are used to disentangling massive complexity in all our performing arts and can enjoy the sound of large and small ensembles as a cultural norm. In the Middle Ages a solo recital was largely what was expected. Entertainment would be provided by a solo harpist, a solo crowther (crwth player; a crwth is a bowed lyre), or perhaps a singer who accompanied him- or herself or sang unaccompanied. This may explain why several instruments carry within their design what we may call 'self-accompaniment'. The crwth (or 'crowd', as the English translated that Welsh name) probably had a flat rather than a curved bridge. The crowther would play a melody on one string with the others providing a drone. When the Old French poet Beroul, in his late-twelfth-century account of the tale of Tristan, refers to the musicians, is he implying a wind band or is he simply saying that, one after another, a host of musicians lined up to give solo recitals? The poem does not answer the question beyond doubt. (A calomel is a reed pipe and a troine is another musical instrument – perhaps a kind of shawm, for this is out of doors.)

'Maint calomel, mainte troine
Qui fu la nuit en la gaudine
Ouist en pavellon soner.'

('If you had been there that night in the woods you would have heard many a pipe and many a shawm playing in the pavilion.')

Beroul, *Roman de Tristan*

Take the bagpipe, which we find in numerous pictures. For us, bagpipes tend to be associated with Burns Night Suppers and Black Watch parades. But in medieval Europe they were to be found all over the place. Modern enthusiasts have seized on fragmentary information to reconstruct Welsh, English, Cornish and other bagpipes. We certainly know that there were various kinds of English ones: for a start, anyone peering under the tip-up seats in a cathedral choir is likely to find a carved bagpiper somewhere. For another bagpiper, most famously, we turn to the Miller in Chaucer's *Canterbury Tales*: when the pilgrims leave London it is he who pipes them out of town.

> 'A whit cote and a blew hood wered he.
> A baggepipe wel koude he blowe and sowne,
> And therwithal he broughte us out of towne.'

> ('He wore a white coat and a blue hood. He was very good at playing the bagpipe and that's how he accompanied us as we left town.')

> Chaucer, General Prologue to *The Canterbury Tales*

Why did Chaucer pick bagpipes for his character? Chaucer was not a novelist. He dealt in vigorously described types, rather than characters in the sense of those found in Tolstoy's or George Eliot's novels. So may we assume that competence on bagpipes was typical of millers in medieval England? Well, it is possible – but perhaps Chaucer simply wanted us to conclude that his Miller was loud and vulgar! Literary evidence, as with Beroul, is hard to use with confidence.

As we have already seen, there is little concrete information when it comes to the instrumentation of medieval music. But there are exceptions: Machaut (c. 1300–1377) was one of the few composers to leave us clear instructions about the intended performance of a piece. In his poem *Le Voir Dit*, he explains that the work, written for his lover Peronne, should be performed without ornamentation, and that in addition to being sung it may be played on the organ – or bagpipes.

Recordings of medieval and early Renaissance instrumental music should not be dismissed as an uninformed modern take on the repertoire. But it would be equally rash to assume that they are academically watertight reconstructions. A competent musical barrister could cut a swathe through these recordings, and any other instrumental performances of this music, because there is not sufficient evidence for such certainty; yet we have too much evidence to ignore the topic! That's why several generations of musicians have sifted through the evidence that we do have, formed their own ideas and put them into practice. And although universities echo to the sound of continuing scholarly argument, we would all be much the poorer not to see the theories tested in the only proper manner: in performance. The website offers two pieces both in contrasting versions to illustrate the decision-making process: Josquin's little Renaissance song *El grillo* `website 15-16` and Landini's fourteenth-century *Non avrà ma'pietà questa mia donna* `website 10-11`. The differences between the two performances of each piece are much more marked than the similarities, which illustrates the extent to which our experience of early music is determined by the performers.

VI. Towards the Renaissance

Polyphony

Polyphony was the avant-garde of the Middle Ages. Indeed, this music, in which more than one part is playing at the same time, is so cutting-edge that many people today associate it more with the Renaissance. Yet it began simply enough, as an embellishment of plainchant, as was explained in two music treatises written as early as the ninth century. This decorated plainchant progresses with additional parts, which still largely shadow the chant line, moving with it but at a fixed interval's distance. When it goes up, they go up (and by the same amount), and when it goes down, they do too. This technique is known as organum, but somewhat confusingly the word meant more than one thing in the Middle Ages. It could sometimes mean an organ, for a start; it could also mean various kinds of song or psalm, and even the Psalter as a whole. For our purposes, though, organum is music in which a part is added above or below a plainchant line (which is called the *cantus firmus*, meaning 'fixed song'). In the earliest examples, the parts moved at the same speed and the interval between them did not vary: from this it got the name 'parallel organum'. In addition, there developed music in which melismas (see glossary) were sung above the long chant syllables. As the two approaches divided, the older-style syllabic form, where the two melodies proceeded together in exact step, note for note, became known as discant; this left the freer, melismatic style to be known as organum, or 'melismatic organum', as it is called today for clarity.

The place with which organum is most closely associated is the cathedral of Notre Dame in Paris, home of the great twelfth-century composer Léonin (*fl.* 1150– c. 1201) and his successor Pérotin (*fl.* c. 1200) (the job changed hands around 1180). Large quantities of music were written for the newly built establishment. Léonin is thought both to have compiled the *Magnus liber organi* ('Great Book of Organum'), which is the collection of polyphony for Notre Dame Cathedral in Paris, and to have written part of it himself (listen to *Viderunt omnes* website 4). This is a substantial collection of music, enough for the entire church year. That we know about Léonin (and to a large extent Pérotin) at all is down to a thirteenth-century English commentator known to us only as 'Anonymous IV'. It was he who recorded that Léonin was a great composer of organum who compiled a substantial book of Mass settings and Office chants used at Notre Dame. For Léonin's music we are dependent on copies made in the thirteenth century, but these give no names and leave us unsure when the music in the manuscripts was actually composed. Anonymous IV also tells us that Pérotin revised the *Magnus liber*, which implies that he either edited or rewrote his predecessor's music – if so, we have little chance of knowing who wrote what. However, there is enough evidence to be clear that Pérotin wrote in the emerging discant style, even though we cannot be sure whether the older Léonin did. Anonymous IV certainly calls Léonin the greatest composer of organum and Pérotin the greatest composer of discant.

In the latter part of twelfth century, a system of six rhythmic patterns came into being. Both discant and organum continued to develop. Organum remained unrhythmicised, but the breakaway style of the *ars antiqua* (or 'old art', distinguishing it from the later 'new art' of the fourteenth century) adapted to the new rhythms. Next, the upper part was given a different text from the lower chant line – and this marked the beginning of the motet. By the start of the thirteenth century, composers like Pérotin were writing large-scale works in which the plainchant line consisted of held notes (this line that holds on tenaciously is where we get the word 'tenor' from), while two or even three different lines were sung above it in a fast rhythmicised polyphony.

This was also the time when the new Gothic style of architecture swept across Europe and eclipsed the preceding Romanesque style, resulting in cathedrals that opted for fluted columns rather than powerful solid piers, and pointed arches over rounded ones. It was a style that emphasised the height of buildings. In England can be found several examples of cathedrals (notably Canterbury) where you can see the two styles side by side, as the building work took so long that fashions changed during the construction process, with the builders moving over to the new style halfway through.

The Motet

The motet is probably the single most important polyphonic genre of the Middle Ages. This was the genre, above all, in which composers displayed both learning and imagination. It also created the musical future: without the medieval motet there could have been no Renaissance madrigal. For the first 200 years of its life, the motet structure was as follows: at the bottom, there was a plainchant tenor line with a Latin text, sung slowly; sitting on top of this were one or more higher voices, singing texts that were not only different and unrelated but could even be in a different language from the chant.

The motet was fundamentally a polytextual song, i.e., different lines set different texts. That was the case up until Dufay in the 1440s, by which time we really are knocking on the door of the Renaissance. He was one of the most highly praised of fifteenth-century composers and is represented here by a *chanson*, *Adieu ces bons vins de Lannoys* website 9 . Guillaume Dufay (1397–1474) was certainly prolific: as well as eight complete settings of the Mass, and several hymns and single movements from the Mass, we also know of eighty-four songs. This music is famous for its warmth, clarity and expressiveness, and you may well feel when listening to it that the Renaissance has already begun.

The key *formes fixes* ('fixed forms') of medieval France were three types of song: the *rondeau*, *ballade* and *virelai*. All three started out as monophonic song forms, although these names defined verse forms as well as musical structures, and there were different regular patterns of textual and musical repetition which distinguished them. Although they were secular songs, when Pope Clement V moved from Rome to Avignon in France (sparking outrage in Rome and startling Christendom) his court became a centre of excellence for these compositions.

The New Art

Guillaume de Machaut (c. 1300–1377) was a priest and a poet as well as a composer. He worked for King John of Bohemia in Prague and Paris, and he followed the monarch on a number of military expeditions across Europe until John died at the hands of the English at Crécy in 1346. Machaut is one of the most famous composers of the Middle Ages, not least because he took care to leave manuscripts of his works in good order. As a result, over 140 of his compositions have come down to us. These include pieces both in the older monophonic traditions of *virelais* and *lais*, and the newer, more melismatic and rhythmically varied polyphonic style. In this respect he shows himself both the heir of the *trouvère* tradition of song and a man of his times. In fact, his continued use of traditional forms earned him the title of 'the last of the trouvères'. Despite being a cleric, however, he wrote little church music.

During the early fourteenth century, a more complex musical style grew up. This was given the name *ars nova* ('new art') by the French composer and theorist Philippe de Vitry (1291–1361), and Machaut was its most famous practitioner. For some music historians, the arrival of the *ars nova* heralds the arrival of the Renaissance.

The *ars nova* composers set out to find the means of

Guillaume de Machaut (c. 1300–1377)

writing larger-scale works than monophonic songs. They were in part responding to the consequences of the development of organum (rather like Schoenberg thinking through the logical development of music while studying the richness yet inherent weakness being exposed by the developments in late Romanticism). The *cantus firmus* was no longer capable of holding the piece together: the demands being made on it were so great that it was being distorted and thus was less useful as a unifying principle. Machaut and his contemporaries responded by imposing a regular, repeating rhythmic pattern on the tenor line. This is called a *talea*. This principle of unity through repetition, or isorhythm (from the Greek *iso*, 'same'), may be familiar to anyone used to playing or hearing a ground bass – the repeating bass line that is such a feature of Baroque music. But a *talea* is less easily detected than a ground bass, for the simple reason that its cycles are longer. Moreover, the principle of repetition was sometimes used to create two repeating lines, different from one another and out of phase.

Isorhythmically organised voice parts were used to form the foundation for large works, and other melodies could be laid over them to produce a polyphonic result more intricate and complex than anything previously possible. As with all artistic revolutions, what is new and different may be what strikes us first; but on further investigation change usually turns out to be built on a strong basis of continuity. So it is with *ars nova*: much may be new but the foundation voice, or *cantus firmus*, is usually taken from plainchant. The new compositional approach fed particularly into the developing genre of the motet, and in a new spirit of confidence in complexity, some motets not only boasted isorhythms but set several different texts to be sung simultaneously. One distinctive feature of *ars nova* was the attention given to secular music. The unharmonised melodies that had been sung in the thirteenth century by the troubadours and *trouvères* were expanded by fourteenth-century composers into two- and three-voice pieces called *chansons* (songs). We find increasing numbers of these songs being written in different forms, all defined by specific patterns of rhyme and musical repetition: *rondeau*, *virelai* and *ballade* in France, and madrigal, *caccia* and *balata* in Italy.

The practice also developed of giving prominence to the *cantus*, or top line, of a composition in several parts: the principal melodic interest would be in the highest voice, leaving the other vocal or instrumental parts in a supporting role. This, of course, was reversing what happened in organum, where the lower line contained the principal musical activity and the upper lines were a kind of accompanying decoration on it (like the descant line that sometimes adorns hymns in modern church singing).

Ars nova also influenced music written for the Mass. Up until the end of the thirteenth century, the use of polyphony in the Mass had been restricted to particular sections. In the fourteenth century, all the sections that make up the Ordinary of the Mass (Kyrie, Gloria, Credo, Sanctus, Benedictus, Agnus Dei) began to be treated as an integrated whole. The first person to do this, as far as we know, was Guillaume de Machaut.

Dunstable and Simplicity

Every new generation rebels against what has gone before. In the early fifteenth century, composers reacted against the growing complexity of music. John Dunstable was seen as the leader of a new style, in which composers opted for a simpler music with graceful melodies and smooth harmonies (listen to *Veni Creator* website 12). One voice part now tended to act as a principal melody with the others in an accompanying role.

Dunstable or Dunstaple (c. 1385–1453) is one of Britain's greatest composers. If, as we think, he was born at the end of the fourteenth century and died midway through the fifteenth, his life would have spanned the late stages of the wars against France and the early stages of the Wars of the Roses. Dunstable is a Bedfordshire town, and there is evidence linking the composer to the Duke of Bedford. It may be that Dunstable accompanied the duke to France when that noble was the regent, during the minority of Henry VI.

Sorting out how much of the surviving English music from this period is actually by Dunstable is a tricky process. He was highly regarded by his contemporaries and this meant that works by other composers were often attributed to him. Such a high level of uncertainty makes establishing the chronology of his works, let alone pursuing any useful discussion of style and structure, painfully difficult. It is feasible to analyse English music of the fifteenth century, but pinpointing exactly what it was that made Dunstable so esteemed by his contemporaries is almost impossible. Yet esteemed he certainly was. For anyone who has grown up with the notion that the history of English music is a bit of a national embarrassment – a (not entirely deserved) reputation based on a paucity of great composers between Purcell and Elgar – it is salutary to read fifteenth-century accounts describing how Dunstable influenced Binchois, Busnois, Dufay, Ockeghem and others.

Missa 'L'homme armé'

Robert Morton (1430–after 1479) was from a later generation of English composers, and is deservedly far less famous than Dunstable. Morton, an Englishman who worked as a member of the Burgundian chapel from 1457 to 1475, nevertheless demands our attention as the probable composer of the hit song of the age: *L'homme armé*. This *chanson* about 'beware the armed man' somehow achieved unparalleled popularity with composers. There is no obvious answer to why it became so popular. Certainly it is simple and catchy, has a very clear structure, and can be used as a canon: this all allows it to be easily manipulated and elaborated upon. Busnois, Dufay, Josquin, Obrecht, Ockeghem, Palestrina and others all made use of it in what are called parody Masses (that is, Masses using an existing melody). (A seventeenth-century Mass by Carissimi, a twentieth-century one by Karl Jenkins and a twenty-first-century one by Peter Maxwell Davies may also be added to the list.) As with John Taverner's *In nomine*, of which more later, it is difficult to account for its immense popularity.

Medieval or Renaissance

By now, a major question presents itself. Of all the composers at this point – Dunstable, Machaut, Dufay, Binchois,

Guillaume Dufay (1397–1474) and
Gilles Binchois (c. 1400–1460)

Ockeghem, Josquin, Janequin *et al.* – how do we decide which of them is medieval and which Renaissance? Does the sound of *D'ung aultre amer* `website 13` by Johannes Ockeghem (c. 1410–1479), here using a countertenor voice accompanied by viol ensemble, have the qualities that art historians can find in the paintings of his contemporary Masaccio (1401–c. 1428)? Is the music of Antoine Busnois (c. 1430–1492) – such as *Alleluya* `website 14` – sufficiently polyphonic and sophisticated (or too French, too Burgundian and not Italian enough) for him to be classed as a Renaissance composer? What would we be looking for anyway, if we tried to form such a definition of Renaissance music, separating it from what went before? The abandonment of the late-medieval complexity of isorhythms and the movement towards a simpler and more lyrical melodic line, perhaps? The matching increase in rhythmic simplicity with the tendency of composers to use less syncopation? Do these attributes correspond to the move in painting towards a greater sense of the whole and away from the accumulation of intricate detail? Or does Renaissance music by contrast involve the skilful handing of complex material?

Perhaps we should in fact look towards the late-fifteenth century's polyphonic sacred music (the Masses of Ockeghem and Obrecht). In this new contrapuntalism all the parts stem from a single musical line and might reflect the Renaissance ability to impose order on a work of art so that every detail is a servant to the total conception. It is not easy to be precise about such things, which is why scholars disagree. But it is reasonable to say that when music began to rely heavily on imitation (the tightly spaced restatement of the same melodic idea in different parts) as a principal structural element, then it was on its way into the Renaissance. So where you have Renaissance composers, you are soon going to find canonic music – music with rolling, overlapping imitations of a melody (similar to the effect you can hear in *Three Blind Mice* or *London's Burning*).

Certainly Josquin des Prez (c. 1450/55–c. 1521) was regarded as a Renaissance composer in his lifetime, being compared then (and since) with Michelangelo. A pupil of Ockeghem and teacher of Janequin, he was praised by Martin Luther and he worked for the powerful Medici family. He is represented here by a tiny song called *El grillo* ('The Cricket') website 15-16 , performed in two highly contrasting versions, and by part of the Mass 'La sol fa re mi' website 17 .

It is noticeable that the musical centre of gravity was Burgundy (then covering parts of what is now northern France and Belgium), which is why so many of the great musicians of the time are described as being 'Franco-Flemish'. The Burgundian court at the time of the English Wars of the Roses was one of the wonders of the age: indeed, it is the focus of one of the seminal books on this period, *The Waning of the Middle Ages*, by Johan Huizinga. For Huizinga, this time and place are best understood as the apogee of a period in cultural history rather than the dawning of a new one; one of the marks of that achievement is the enormous wealth of Franco-Flemish composers. But there was another place besides Burgundy that held enormous importance for composers, and that was Italy.

Josquin des Prez (c. 1450/55–c. 1521)

VII. What Was the Renaissance?

Anyone looking in a history book or dictionary will discover that our word 'renaissance' is of French derivation and means 'rebirth'. So clearly the word is referring to a belief that something was alive, then died and was reborn. Italian Renaissance writers certainly felt that this had happened. Figures such as the fourteenth-century poet Petrarch and the sixteenth-century artist and art critic Vasari (another Florentine) argued that there had been a peak of perfection in human activity during the time of the ancient Greeks and Romans followed by a total collapse during the Middle Ages, and that their own time had seen the arrival of a new peak of perfection. In fact, this was when the expression 'Middle Ages' itself first started to be used to describe the valley between these two heights of human achievement. A key element in the Renaissance's understanding of itself was its devotion to Greek and Roman ideals in the arts and in thought. Of course, Latin had been universally used throughout the Middle Ages among scholars; but they had almost without exception been members of the Church. (Greek was less familiar and its literature often only known through Latin translations, adaptations and descriptions.) But the Renaissance saw a new attempt to think like Classical philosophers, which meant thinking like non-Christian philosophers.

There is another way of looking at the Renaissance: to observe how the term itself is used. Usually when people today use the word 'renaissance', it turns out to mean 'a lot of high-quality activity going on in a short space of time and usually in a particular place'. Take, for example, the 'Harlem Renaissance'. There may be some suggestion that African-Americans were rediscovering a creativity and confidence they had possessed since the transatlantic slave trade had removed them from Africa: that's the 'rebirth' element in the name. But beyond that, it really means that a lot of people were writing poetry and playing jazz, and different art forms were developing rapidly in a specific time and place.

As we've already discovered, it's very difficult to impose precise dates on historical periods. Some scholars and poets are referred to as 'Italian humanists' from as early as 1300: Dante, for example, and Petrarch. Since humanism is one of the defining marks of the Renaissance, does this imply that we should stop referring to music as 'medieval' from that point? The early fourteenth century certainly saw the development of a new musical style. The complex, polyphonic manner of *ars nova* was matched by a developing use of notation around 1300. But in contrast to what was happening in literature and the visual arts, this movement was not being driven either by a sense of the revival of classical Rome or by Italian masters. In fact, *ars nova* came from France and for that reason alone might be better thought of as a medieval musical style, since France saw itself (and was usually seen) as the cultural engine of medieval western Europe. Indeed, while this development affected both secular and sacred music in France it seems to have reached Italy only in around 1330. Thereafter, there was a fashion for Italian composers to set French texts.

Of course, a medievalist analysing what was going on in Renaissance Europe might readily conclude that any changes were heavily outweighed by a sense of continuity. On the military–diplomatic front, the struggle for power in Italy that had been encountered by Charlemagne in 800 and Dante in 1300 remained a central feature of life: the French kings Charles VIII and Francis I both invaded and won victories. There was still discussion of the Islamic threat and talk of a new Crusade to free the Holy Places, though this came to little. And no one at the time was entirely convinced that late-medieval wars such as the Wars of the Roses in England or the Hundred Years War between England and France were really over: rebellions that might have tilted over into new outbreaks of civil war continued to trouble England right through into the sixteenth century. Edward IV and Henry VII both mounted invasions of France, although it is true to say that neither of them was at all serious about reconquering vast tracts of it: some historians have regarded the invasions less as a military matter and more a fund-raising scheme, exploiting the rules that allowed kings to impose taxes to pay for wars. Nevertheless, despite the friendly meeting between Henry VIII and Francis I at the famous 'Field of the Cloth of Gold' (actually a diplomatic necessity for Francis to protect his back before invading Italy), disputes over the Plantagenet–Angevin inheritance in mainland Europe likewise continued into the mid-sixteenth century. It was only during the reign of Mary I that the last piece of England's

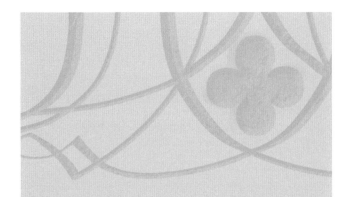

Niccolò Machiavelli guaranteed his place in the history books with the publication of his controversial and hard-hitting book *The Prince*, written to advise rulers how to protect their kingdoms at a time when Italy was frequently invaded by foreign powers. As he explains here, it was essential to be cruel to be kind:

'A prince must want to have a reputation for compassion rather than for cruelty: nonetheless, he must be careful that he does not make bad use of compassion. Cesare Borgia was accounted cruel; nevertheless this cruelty of his reformed the Romagna, brought it unity, and restored order and obedience. On reflection, it will be seen that there was more compassion in Cesare than in the Florentine people, who, to escape being called cruel, allowed Pistoia to be devastated. So a prince must not worry if he incurs reproach for his cruelty so long as he keeps his subjects united and loyal. By making an example or two he will prove more compassionate than those who, being too compassionate, allow disorders which lead to murder and rapine. These nearly always harm the whole community, whereas executions ordered by a prince only affect individuals.'

medieval empire was finally lost, to her profound political embarrassment.

However, on other fronts, there *were* changes. An improvement in the manufacture of paper, notably cheaper than the older parchment, meant that it was adopted for most everyday business. The discovery and development of printing reduced the cost of books and helped to support an expansion of secular literacy, because driving down the cost meant driving up the availability of books – including books of music. Scholars have concluded that composers of the new music took for granted and exploited the existence of notation in the way in which they composed (i.e., the level of detail and complexity in this music would not have been possible to communicate to the performers without notation), and that increasingly music was also affected by the growth in literacy. Developments in modern music were thus being supported and encouraged by developments in modern technology, a phenomenon that we have also seen in our own times.

This was very much a period of expansion and discovery. The large migrations of peoples – from Goths to Crusaders – that had marked the Middle Ages were largely over, except at the margins, where people such as reindeer herders in Europe's farthest north continued their traditional way of life. The Crusade in Portugal and Spain finally ended with the conquest of the last Muslim kingdom in 1492. Instead, there was a move in new directions and using a new (or at least newly extended) means of transport. During the fifteenth century, Europeans sailed south until they rounded the most distant point of Africa, the Cape of Good Hope. They also reached India by a sea route for the first time; they sailed west until they discovered the West Indies; they reached Brazil, sailed around Cape Horn, and discovered the Pacific Ocean. Europeans had travelled great distances before and seen new worlds: Alexander the Great had fought his way to India two millennia earlier, and medieval missionaries had journeyed to China, astonishingly enough, and established a church there that flourished for some time. But sea voyages of this number and magnitude had no precedent, even in the great days of Viking exploration. For the first time, European people were beginning to have an understanding of the totality of the globe.

Given the nature of the times, it is hardly surprising that a discussion grew up about what the lost music of Greece and Rome had been like, and how it might be recreated. We know that sixteenth-century Italian sculptors would rush to see newly discovered Roman remains: Michelangelo and the unearthed Apollo Belvedere, for example. Scholars would excitedly correspond, as we know from surviving letters, discussing documents that they had come upon in libraries. However, since no Roman music of any kind was then (or indeed is now) available, rediscovery was not possible; it was therefore a matter of imaginative reinvention. But in fact, 'reinvention' seems largely to have taken the form of continuing with the developments that the late Middle Ages had set in train – that is, polyphony and the madrigal. Of course there were debates about Greek modes, and there were attempts to experiment with scales in order to try to resurrect Greek musical structures. Even today, despite all our archaeology and scientific method, we know very little about Greek and Roman music. Nevertheless, we know enough to

In this eyewitness account of the Spanish conquest of Mexico, written by one of Hernándo Cortés's captains, we are given a vivid picture of the thrill and the fear experienced by Renaissance explorers:

'Early next day we left Iztapalapa with a large escort of these great caciques, and followed the causeway, which is eight yards wide and goes so straight to the city of Mexico that I do not think it curves at all; wide though it was, it was so crowded with people that there was hardly room for them all. Some were going to Mexico and others coming away, besides those who had come out to see us, so we could hardly get through the crowds that were there. For the towers and the cues were full and they came in canoes from all parts of the lake. No wonder, since they had never seen horses or men like us before!

With such wonderful sights to gaze on we did not know what to say, or if this was real that we saw before our eyes. On the land side there were great cities and on the lake many more. The lake was crowded with canoes. At intervals along the causeway there were many bridges, and before us was the great city of Mexico. As for us, we were scarcely four hundred strong, and we well remembered the words and warnings of the people of Huexotzinco and Tlaxcala and Tlamanalco, and the many other warnings we had received to beware of entering the city of Mexico, since they would kill us as soon as they had us inside. Let the interested reader consider whether there is not much to ponder in this narrative of mind. What men in all the world have shown such daring?'

say that the idea of a 'rebirth' would have had the very opposite effect to the one the Renaissance composers wanted. Theirs was a polyphonic age, while Greeks and Romans had almost certainly been entertained by monophonic music – music which was therefore a great deal more like that of the secular Middle Ages than what came out of the Renaissance.

There's no question, though, that there was a lot of high-quality activity going on, plus a lot of high-level excitement and experiment, which certainly indicates that music participated in the Renaissance in at least the second sense offered earlier. In addition, there was another change that fits in with the definition of 'renaissance' – the increasing importance of the secular world. We have already found that compared with vocal and sacred, little secular and instrumental music of the Middle Ages has come down to us. By contrast, Renaissance composers took secular music seriously enough to compose and notate a good deal of it. The breakthrough made by Ottaviano Petrucci in 1501 of printing music from movable type helped this development.

VIII. The Renaissance Madrigal

The madrigal originated in fourteenth-century secular songs, such as the two-part compositions by Francesco Landini (c. 1325–1397). You can hear some of his music on ⟨website 10.11⟩, where a vocal and a purely instrumental account of essentially the same piece make a striking contrast. By the time of the Renaissance, the madrigal had become a polyphonic song intent on bringing out the character of the words set. Carlo Gesualdo (c. 1561–1613) was unusual among composers in being of noble birth. A Neapolitan prince, he had no need to seek work or please a patron. His nobility also helped him to evade punishment when, in a fit of jealous rage, he murdered his wife after discovering her with her lover. It is tempting to link what we know of this tempestuous life with what we hear of his music, for it was daringly chromatic, using notes that even to our modern ears can sound strange and sometimes 'wrong' (listen for example to his *Tribulationem et dolorem* ⟨website 32⟩). He was not alone in this, enriching the music but making it more confusing as well as more exciting. The madrigal was a genre which emphasised emotion and the musical expression of the subject: if the subject was passion (and it often was), composers would naturally reach for the emotionally strenuous language of chromaticism. Examples can be found in the work of Luzzasco Luzzaschi (?1545–1607) and Alfonso Fontanelli (1557–1622), with both of whose music Gesualdo was certainly familiar, and the later work of Luca Marenzio (c. 1553–1599), as it became increasingly preoccupied with death.

The madrigal was a highly successful musical genre. Developed in the late Middle Ages, it held the interest and enthusiasm of composers and audiences right through the Renaissance and into the Baroque period, where it flourished in the hands of composers such as Claudio Monteverdi (1567–1643). We shouldn't be surprised by this, for Monteverdi inherited the Renaissance dream of recreating the lost musical glories of Greece and Rome. Like others of his time, he meditated on the nature of Greek tragic theatre, with its inimitable mixture of drama, dance and music, and, in attempting to write works that followed that model, effectively created opera.

However, even before the development of opera, there was a widespread fascination with classical Greek and Roman subjects. Of course medieval writers had certainly written about classical subjects such as the Trojan War, but there was little tradition of painting classical subjects in the Middle Ages or writing songs with classical themes. The English consort song was a close cousin to the developing Renaissance theatre, sometimes being a spin-off from plays and masques. William Byrd is remembered primarily as a composer of sacred music, but he also wrote theatre songs: *Quis me statim* was probably originally written for a performance at Christ

Church, Oxford in 1592 of Seneca's *Hippolytus*, a Roman play with its own origins in an ancient Greek masterpiece.

One of the most notable aspects of madrigals and consort songs was that the voice was treated as an instrument: they could be sung *a cappella* or with instruments, but they were true ensemble pieces, with all parts having equal importance. Even if instruments were used the voice often took the top line, but there are still some examples of a descant being played above the vocal line, on a viol.

In France, the *chanson* was essentially the same as the madrigal, although the texts were less impassioned. Instead, composers sought to charm and delight the listener. Clément Janequin (c. 1485–after 1558), a pupil of Josquin, is famous for his programme music – songs in which specific subjects are dramatised. *La Guerre*, for example, is a musical picture of the Battle of Marignano (1515: it was a notable event of those long-running Italian wars in which emperors and popes were both embroiled), depicting the clash of swords and battle cries. Janequin's *Le Chant des oiseaux* (website 18) conveys birdsong, and his *Voulez ouier les cris de Paris?* imitates a city street complete with itinerant vendors plying their trade. Singers variously sing, shout, use nonsense syllables and coo like birds. (All three topics were taken up by other composers, and there is a minor tradition of battles and birds in music that includes works by Beethoven, Messiaen and even Pablo Casals.)

Accompanying this rise in the importance allotted to secular music was an increase in the level of literacy. Far more rulers could read and write than had been the case in the Middle Ages, where the literacy of English kings Alfred and

Henry VIII (1491–1547)

John was a matter of comment. Kings and princes took pride in being literate and in being able to play a musical instrument; Henry VIII (1491–1547) and Pope Leo X (1475–1521) both composed music of their own. Musicians were better paid and more highly respected, and their passing more profoundly mourned than previously. Lorenzo de' Medici ensured that the Medici musician Antonio di Bartolomeo Squarcialupi, the son of a butcher and the most famous organist of his day, was given a memorial in the Florentine chapel where the Medici family prayed. Emperor Maximilian knighted his court organist Paul Hofheimer. When Ockeghem died in 1485, the great Erasmus wrote an epitaph for him. Ironically, the one song that most people believe to have been composed by Henry VIII, *Greensleeves*, wasn't his work at all. On the other hand, *Pastime with good company* does appear to be his, albeit more an arrangement of a Flemish source than an entirely new composition. Henry's musicianship is celebrated in a miniature in a Latin psalter where he is the model for a portrait of King David the Psalmist. (The picture shows the King playing a small harp, with his entertainer Will Sommers listening and wringing his hands in some apparent distress; perhaps he had perfect pitch and the monarch did not!)

IX. Europe Divided

We should not forget that while the Renaissance developed in
Italy, its cousin the Reformation was starting in Germany.
Throughout the later Middle Ages there had been academic
debates and political rows about how to reform the Roman
Catholic Church. Everyone agreed that it needed reforming,
but no one could agree how. The problem was that virtually
everyone involved in the debate was an interested party,
which meant that they all had something to lose. In the end,
one campaigner, a German monk called Martin Luther
(1483–1546), became a rallying point for reform; the
Reformation finally began on 31 October 1517 when he
nailed his ninety-five theses to the door of the castle church in
Wittenberg, without Roman and Papal approval but instead
with the sponsorship of a number of local secular rulers. This
action had dramatic and long-lasting effects. For one thing, it
split Europe as profoundly as had the Great Schism, the
division of the church between a Catholic west and Orthodox
east which had been in effect formalised in 1054. Worse, it
split individual countries. In England, the Henrician
Reformation was set in train by Henry VIII, himself an amateur
theologian as well as a composer.

England's second Tudor king, Henry had come to power a Roman Catholic and had married the devoutly Catholic Spanish princess who would have been his older brother's queen but for Prince Arthur's untimely death. When Catherine of Aragon proved unable to have more than one child (and a girl at that, which was undesirable at a time when any perceived weakness of the monarchy might trigger a renewal of civil war), and when a young woman educated at the French court turned out to be pretty and sharp-witted, Henry demanded a divorce. The only person who could give him one – the Pope – was at the time in no position to hand one out, being effectively the political prisoner of the queen's nephew. Things then reached a critical pass: Anne Boleyn was pregnant, and Henry was not about to give up what looked like the possibility of an heir being born to him at last. Henry's eventual divorce was, as a result, a kind of do-it-yourself job that ensued from a Unilateral Declaration of Independence from Roman power, based – in the best Renaissance tradition – on obscure medieval precedents. The result was that for the rest of the sixteenth century England alternated between having a government which persecuted Protestants (under the young Henry VIII and his second heir) and one which persecuted Catholics (under the older Henry VIII and his first and third heirs).

For example, in the reign of Elizabeth I (Henry VIII's second surviving child and the daughter of the woman for whom he had divorced his first wife) there remained a notable (although how large it is difficult to be sure) Roman Catholic community which may well have believed it was only a matter of time before England returned to the Church it had, after all, only left by accident. At the same time, Elizabeth's older sister (and predecessor as monarch) Mary I was married to the devout Spanish king Philip II, one of the most powerful political and military figures in Europe and considered in some quarters to be the true king of England, since he was the dead queen's widower and Elizabeth had been declared illegitimate by the Catholics. With that threat constantly hanging over the regime, Catholics were in danger of being seen as potential traitors: rather like communists in Cold War America, the fear was that their first loyalty would be not to their country but to a supranational organisation.

Similarly, there were others who were the Protestant equivalent of ultra-loyalists. One of these is said to have been John Taverner (c. 1490–1545), a composer and organist. Born in Lincolnshire, he worked in a church in Tattershall in the 1520s before becoming, in 1526, the choirmaster at Cardinal's College, Oxford (so called because it had been founded by Cardinal Thomas Wolsey; it was renamed Christ Church after his fall from power). Taverner seems to have got mixed up in Lutheranism and was imprisoned for heresy in 1528. He left the college in 1530, following Wolsey's fall, and became a lay clerk at the parish church of St Botolph in Boston, Lincolnshire, remaining there until his death in 1545. There is a persistent legend that Taverner gave up music to become an agent in the service of Thomas Cromwell, Wolsey's secretary, and later the driving political force behind the break with Rome and the subsequent attack on church institutions. Taverner is also said to have been part of the team that forced through the dissolution of the monasteries.

Scholars believe that most of Taverner's surviving work is from the 1520s. He wrote several settings of the Mass and of the Magnificat, and a number of motets, but his 'Western Wynde' Mass, using the melody from a then-popular song, is perhaps his best-known sacred work. His younger contemporary Christopher Tye (c. 1505–?1573) was a member of King's College Chapel Choir as a boy who went on to do a BMus at the university and become choirmaster at Ely Cathedral. He later moved to the Chapel Royal, where he was organist; legend has it that Queen Elizabeth I would sometimes send through a message that he was playing out of tune. According to the seventeenth-century Oxford historian and biographer Anthony Wood, Tye would respond by sending a message back telling Her Royal Highness that, on the contrary, her ears were out of tune. Like Taverner (and John Sheppard, c. 1515–1558), Tye wrote a parody Mass based on the 'Western Wynde' tune.

A fragment of the Benedictus from Taverner's Mass 'Gloria tibi Trinitas' was arranged for an instrumental consort by the composer himself. Many others then also made arrangements of the fragment, and an entirely new genre of English consort music developed: the *In nomine* `website 22-23`. Taking its name from the words of the Mass text ('In nomine Domini' – 'In the name of the Lord'), it was a genre that embraced both consort and keyboard compositions.

Harder to place in the religious politics of the day is Thomas Tallis (c. 1505–1585), perhaps best known today through Vaughan Williams's *Fantasia on a Theme of Thomas Tallis*. He worked as an organist in various locations, including Waltham Abbey in Essex. When the dissolution of

Thomas Tallis (c. 1505–1585)

the abbey in 1540 as part of the break-up of Roman Catholic theological and socio-economic structures made Tallis redundant, he got a job as a lay clerk at Canterbury Cathedral before moving to the Chapel Royal in 1543. He served the monarchy until his death, negotiating his way through several changes in the person and religious faith of the head of State. This evidence of individuals' ability to continue in their posts during a period of doctrinal and organisational change is a reminder that the break with Rome did not set in train wholesale change. Henry wanted a divorce and access to the Church's wealth, but he did not want a religious revolution with all the accompanying social upheaval. There were of course some changes, and Protestant influence made itself felt both in church life and musical practice: composers were urged to simplify and clarify music in certain ways. For example, they were encouraged to move away from melismatic, contrapuntal music and towards word-settings which were syllabic and supported by simpler chord sequences. As one can hear in some of Tallis's music (such as his setting of a text from the Old Testament Book of Lamentations), the result was a compromise. There are passages which are polyphonic and marked by a typically Renaissance use of imitation. These contrast with passages which are chordal and in the reformed Anglican spirit. This striving for compromise with the demands of the State might remind us of the problems that Shostakovich faced in Russia, his need to produce music according to his own standards which would nevertheless pass the restrictions imposed by the Communist Party and sometimes even by Stalin himself.

Tallis is said by some scholars to have written *Spem in alium* website 24 following a performance in 1567 of a forty-part work by Alessandro Striggio (c. 1536/37–1592), *Ecce beatam lucem*. Reluctant to be upstaged by the Italians, the Duke of Norfolk challenged English musicians to match Striggio's achievement and Tallis was the one who rose to the occasion. An alternative theory is that he wrote the forty-part motet to mark Queen Elizabeth I's fortieth birthday in 1573. One further privileging of the number forty, discussed below, may make this link with a royal birthday the more likely. The choice of a text from the Book of Judith, in which a woman saves the Israelite nation by slaying a threatening foreign tyrant, may have been intended to flatter the Queen, comparing her defence of Protestantism against the Catholic threat with that of the heroic Judith. But others have intervened in the debate to ask whether Tallis might have actually written the piece to honour her late Catholic majesty Mary I. Scholars do not seem to have noticed a third possibility, which is that there is an allusion to a secret Roman Catholic code by which Holofernes represented the Protestant English State and Judith the avenging true Church. Gregory Martin's *A Treatise of Schism* (1580) certainly made this case, and the belief that the book was also an incitement to assassinate the Queen landed the publisher in trouble with the secret police, leading to his torture and eventual martyrdom.

At this distance it is impossible to be sure of the truth. Perhaps the fact that Tallis was a royal servant in the courts successively of Henry VIII, Edward VI, Mary I and Elizabeth I implies that here was not a man to court controversy; this in turn may suggest that to seek out a politically subversive subtext may be to misread Tallis's character.

The first performance of *Spem in alium* may have been in the banqueting hall of Arundel Castle. This makes sense, since the hall is octagonal, something that would suit the motet's eight choirs (five parts apiece). The opening theme is passed from choir to choir, until finally all forty voices sing together at the climax – which is at the fortieth bar.

Tallis's pupil, friend and business partner William Byrd (c. 1540–1623) was a recusant (or 'refuser') who had to tread a careful path in Elizabethan England, where support for the Catholic Church was seen as implying treasonable support for the Spanish claim to the throne. A deeply pious man, he found both a religious and a musical conflict between his own continuing interest in the (continental, traditional) motet and setting Latin texts for the Roman rite, and the shift in demand towards (English, Anglican) hymns and anthems.

Byrd accordingly kept his head down where possible and even received official patronage. He served under the older Tallis, probably as a choirboy in the Chapel Royal during the reign of Mary I, when the Latin rites of the Catholic Church were restored. He was then appointed organist of Lincoln Cathedral – at the tender age of twenty. He moved (or returned) to the Chapel Royal in 1572 and found himself once again working with Tallis. The two composers were granted a music-printing monopoly by the Elizabeth I; the fact that the petition was submitted in 1573, the year of *Spem in alium*'s first performance, may lend credence to the idea that it was intended to be understood as praise for Elizabeth I. If so, the flattery seems to have worked, for the petition was granted in

William Byrd (c. 1540–1623)

In William Byrd's dedicatory letter in the preface to the first volume of his *Gradualia* (1605), the composer modestly plays down his own role and dwells instead upon the inspiration of the texts themselves:

'I have found there is such a power hidden away and stored up in those words that – I do not know how – to one who meditates upon divine things… all the most fitting melodies come as it were of themselves, and freely present themselves when the mind is alert and eager.'

1575. Later, in 1593, Byrd retired from London altogether, perhaps hoping to avoid being noticed at a time of anti-Catholic anxieties, and went to live at Stondon Massey in Essex – part of a Catholic community that had grown up around the Catholic Petre family of Ingatestone Hall. We are fairly sure that some of his motets were written for this family's private devotions. He also wrote three Latin Masses ⟨website 25⟩ for performance by variously three, four and five single voices. Today scholars and performers often argue about the appropriate number of instruments for use in a piece of medieval music (many? one? none?), or the appropriate number of voices for singing a Bach Passion (one voice per part or a small or large choir?). There cannot be many examples of early music where we are as clear about what an 'authentic' performance should sound like as in these pieces of private religious music by Byrd. Furthermore, whereas the premiere of *Spem in alium* was given in a large hall by a substantial choir, Byrd's Masses were almost certainly first performed in a small private chapel or a room in a private house, by 'two or three, gathered together in my name' as the Gospel of St Matthew puts it.

The Reformation also affected both France and Germany, although in different ways. Hardly had the process of reform been set in train in countries like Germany, Switzerland and the Netherlands than it split into factions. Indeed, Protestants became quite as keen on prosecuting and persecuting one another as the Catholic Church had ever been. While Luther had raised one standard in what is now Germany, John Calvin (1509–1564) had established Geneva as the centre of another kind of Protestantism. Confusingly (at least, for the English!),

Like Byrd, Sir Thomas More was a Catholic. Occupying the post of Lord Chancellor (the equivalent of today's prime minister), he – like Wolsey before him – came to grief over the King's determination to divorce Catherine of Aragon. The story of his refusal to compromise his religious convictions is told in Robert Bolt's play (twice filmed) *A Man for All Seasons*, which draws on a tradition first set down by More's son-in-law William Roper. Here is Roper's account of the saint's end:

'Wherewithal master Pope, takinge his leaue of hym, could not refrayne from wepinge. Which Sir Thomas Moore perceiuinge, comforted him in this wise: "Quiet your self, good master Pope, and be not discomforted; for I trust that we shall, once in heaven, see eche other full merily, where we shalbe sure to live and loue together, in ioyful blisse eternally."

Vppon whose departure, Sir Thomas Moore, as one that had bine invited to some solempne feaste, changed himself into his best apparell; which master Leiuetenaunt espienge, advised him to put it of, sayenge that he that should haue it was but a Javill [rogue].

"What, master Leiuetenaunt," quoth he, "shall I accompte him a Javill that shall doe me this day so singuler a benefitt? Nay, I assure you, were it clothe of gold, I wolde accompt it well bestowed on him, as St Ciprian did, who gaue his executioner thirtie peeces of gould." And albeit at length, throughe master Leiuetenauntes importunate persuasion, he altered his apparell, yeat after thexample of that holy martir St Ciprian, did he, of that litle money that was lefte him, send one Angell of gold to his executioner.

And so was he by master Leiuetenaunte brought out of the Tower, and from thence led towards the place of execution. Where, goinge vppe the scaffold, which was so weake that it was ready to fall, he saide merilye to master Leiuetenaunte: "I pray you, master Leiuetenaunte, see me salf yppe, and for my cominge downe let me shifte for my self."

Then desired he all the people thereaboute to pray for him, and to beare witnes with him that he should nowe there suffer death in and for the faith of the hold chatholik churche. Which done, he kneled downe, and after his prayers said, turned to thexecutioner, and with a cheerefull countenaunce spake thus to him: "Plucke vpp thy spirites, man, and be not afrayde to do thine office; my necke is very shorte; take heede therefore thow strike not awrye, for savinge of thine honestye."

So passed Sir Thomas Moore out of this world to god, vppon the very same daye in which himself had most desired.'

while England largely went with the Lutheran model, Scotland adopted Calvinist practice with consequences that run to this day: the Church of Scotland is Presbyterian and quite distinct from Scotland's Episcopal Church, which is part of the Anglican communion.

In the attempt to cleanse the church, a great deal was destroyed. Throughout the period of religious conflict that ensued from the Reformation statues were defaced, stained glass windows were smashed, and church finery variously burned by reformers or buried by Catholics trying to preserve it for a happier time. The organist in Zurich Cathedral wept as he watched the organ destroyed by those who felt it had no place in a church.

Luther himself was a musician as well as a poet and scholar. He had learned to play the flute and the lute and knew how to compose. And he certainly wasn't afraid to speak his mind on the subject.

> 'He who despises music, as do all the fanatics, does not please me. Music is a gift of God, not a gift of men. Music drives away the Devil and makes people happy... after theology I grant music the highest place and the highest honour.'

He favoured the development of the chorale, a congregational hymn in Protestant Germany, laid out in verses with a repeating melody which the whole congregation could sing. Luther composed several himself, of which the most famous is his *Ein feste Burg ist unser Gott*, sung in English churches as 'A safe stronghold our God is still'. Other composers also set to work. Hans Leo Hassler

(1564–1612) was born in Nuremberg, famous to a later age as the setting for Wagner's *Die Meistersinger*. He studied in Venice and like his contemporary Michael Praetorius (1571–1621) explored both the polyphony that could be heard in Italy and the idea of writing for more two or more choirs singing antiphonally. This chorale tradition led directly to the music of J.S. Bach a century later.

Another composer of the German Reformation was Hans Sachs (1494–1576), the very man who is at the centre of *Die Meistersinger*. A shoemaker by trade, just as the opera shows him, he was a poet and playwright as well as a composer, and he became a follower of Luther. With this link, the 'Meistersinger' music that displaced the earlier 'minnesinger' music (which in turn had its sources in the troubadour movement of the eleventh to thirteenth centuries) flowed into the composition of the new Reformation church songs. Many Protestant hymn tunes derive from the older repertoire.

In France, where the francophone Calvin had the greater influence, the assumption was that church services should consist of biblical texts. Consequently the chorales developed by Luther (and the hymns that were their equivalent in England) were not adopted. Instead, Calvin encouraged the singing of psalms, on the basis that the Book of Psalms was the most ancient set of songs available to the Church. A complete Psalter (i.e., book of Psalms containing music) was published using music variously collected or composed by Louis Bourgeois (c. 1510/15–1559). Four-part harmonisations of the psalms were published by Claude Goudimel (1514/20–1572), who was one of the victims of a massacre of Protestants which took place in Lyon. The great translator of

Father William Weston, a Jesuit priest, describes his mission in a country-house in Berkshire in 1586:

'The place was most suited to our work and ministrations, not merely for the reason that it was remote and had a congenial household, but also because it possessed a chapel, set aside for the celebration of the church's offices. The gentleman was also a skilled musician, and had an organ and other musical instruments and choristers, male and female, [as] members of his household. During these days it was just as if we were celebrating an uninterrupted Octave of some great feast. Mr Byrd, the very famous English musician and organist, was among the company.'

psalms was the poet Clément Marot, who, despite his achievements in the field of metrical psalms and his evident religiosity (combined with a cheerful disposition), nevertheless fell foul of the authorities in Geneva, apparently for wanting to play backgammon on Sundays. Goudimel's setting of Marot's translation of Psalm 130 (website 26) opens with the words 'Du fond de ma pensée', which some will know better in the Latin 'De profundis clamavi' ('From the depths I cry unto Thee'), from which Oscar Wilde took the title of a late autobiographical work, written at the time of his social disgrace and imprisonment.

X. Europe United

It would not be too strong to say that, in terms of the unity of European culture, the Reformation was a disaster. It certainly drove a vast wedge between Protestant and Catholic countries. Of course, Catholic powers initially assumed that this was an aberration and that the schismatic countries would shortly be restored to the main body of the Church: various heresies had been overcome before, and so (they believed) would this one. (A similar, and equally baseless, assumption had reigned for centuries about the schism between the Catholic western and the Orthodox eastern churches.) This conviction that it was merely a matter of time before the rift was healed only fuelled the strife, and two centuries of religious wars began in England, Scotland, France, Germany and elsewhere: the massacre in which the psalmist Goudimel died was but one of many, of which the most famous took place in Paris on St Bartholomew's Day, 1572, during the reign of Charles IX: this event was witnessed by the great English poet Sir Philip Sidney and dramatised for the London stage about two decades later by Christopher Marlowe under the name *The Massacre at Paris*.

Lute Song

Yet despite these conflicts and the suspicion and fear which they bred, there was still an underlying, essentially medieval, sense of European culture. Indeed, just as Dunstable achieved a European reputation, so the songs of John Dowland (1563–1626) were performed across Europe. The lute was arguably the most important domestic instrument at this time, and Dowland was one of the leading lutenists of his age, as well as one of its most remarkable composers. The lute dropped out of favour for some centuries, but a revival of interest in early music has combined with the immense popularity of the guitar to give this sweet-toned instrument a new lease of life. Like the guitar today, it could be played in ensembles, as a solo instrument or to accompany song. Perhaps Dowland's most famous song is *Flow, my tears* (website 28), which he arranged for instruments as the *Lachrymae* (or 'Tears') pavan. Dowland applied for but did not get a job as lutenist at the court of Elizabeth I. Accordingly, he packed his bags and went abroad, travelling around German and Italian courts in the 1590s and obtaining a post at Christian IV's court in Denmark. The tours had helped build his international reputation, and his collections of songs or 'ayres' were warmly received.

Pavan and Galliard

Like being able to sing, being able to dance was an essential social skill in the Renaissance. Indeed, a good deal of secular Renaissance music is dance music, or concert music that uses the forms of dance music. Nothing is more characteristic of

Renaissance England than the pavan and galliard. The pavan is Italian in origin, and its name derives from the word 'paduana', meaning 'dance from Padua'. It was quite a slow court dance in duple time. In contrast, the galliard `website 27` – a variety of 'cinque-pas' or five-step dance – was livelier and in triple time. Music was often put into contrasting pairs or sets of three, and a great deal of music was written for viol consort `website 22/23`, using these two dances as a basic template, even though not all the results were strictly danceable! Sometimes composers chose to make the music so contrapuntal, and the texture therefore so dense, that no dancer could possibly have kept up. These sets of dances were the ancestors of the Baroque suites, which are in turn ancestors of the sonata and the symphony.

Like Dowland, Orlande de Lassus (c. 1532–1594) played a role in the musical histories of several countries, through travel, performance and the adoption of different national styles in his music. Take his name, for example: what should we call him? As well as the accepted form of his name being used here, he is also known in Latin as Orlandus Lassus, in Italian as Orlando di Lasso, and in French as Roland de Lassus; he is often described as a Franco-Flemish composer. But talk of nationality means little in such a case as this. Lassus was born near Mons, made famous as a place of battle in the early part of the First World War; but the political structures that he knew are long since gone, leaving a France that he would not have recognised and a Belgium that did not exist in his day, while the glory that was Burgundy is today a matter of history books and vineyards.

Orlande de Lassus (c. 1532–1594)

Tradition has it that as a boy Lassus had such a beautiful voice that he was kidnapped three times by patrons competing to secure his services. Excelling in every kind of music from an early age, he published both bawdy drinking villanelles and serious madrigals, setting several different languages with equal confidence. Perversely, the breadth of his genius seems to have damaged his modern reputation, leaving Palestrina to emerge as the greatest name of the late Renaissance. Lassus was a master of Masses and motets, madrigals, *chansons* and chorales – for all Europe was his home, and he was at ease in the styles of several different countries. Three highly contrasting pieces by him can be heard on the website [website 33-35].

Heinrich Isaac or Issac (c. 1450/55–1517) is often referred to as a German composer, and he was the doctoral subject of one of the twentieth century's greatest German composers, Anton von Webern. But he is probably better understood as Franco-Flemish, like Lassus, and he worked both in Italy, in the service of that omnipresent Renaissance patron Lorenzo de' Medici, and in Austria, as Maximilian I's court composer between 1497 and 1514. The song *Greiner zancker* [website 29] is played on cornemuse (a reed instrument), lute, fiddle and bass viol accompanying bass, tenor and soprano singers. His contemporary Jacob Obrecht (1457/8–1505) was another product of what was once Burgundy, at a time when it stretched all the way to the sea, and he, too, spent much of his life in Italy. He was a master of both secular and sacred styles. The music on the website – *Stat ('tsaat) ein meskin* [website 30] – is played by two shawms and two sackbuts.

Jacob Obrecht (1457–1508)

Alonso Mudarra (c. 1510–1580) may initially seem a less obvious example of 'Europe United' than well-travelled Franco-Flemish composers who were born in Burgundian lands, worked in Germany, studied in Italy and the like. A Spanish composer, he spent half his life working at Seville Cathedral, as mentioned in Chapter V, but he was a notable composer for the guitar and its cousin, the vihuela. Among the pieces in his *Tres libros de musica en cifras para vihuela* are transcriptions of Franco-Flemish music. He is represented on the website by a small piece, a *Tiento* `website 31`. This literally translates as 'touch', here referring to a free study.

Mudarra's younger contemporary Tomás Luis de Victoria (1548–1611), born in St Theresa's town of Avila, was one of those drawn to Renaissance Italy. Victoria was among the greatest of all Spanish composers. While Lassus was the master of the full range of both sacred and secular genres, Victoria – who may have been a pupil of Palestrina's – was, like Mudarra, a specialist. But whereas the older man wrote for his own instruments, vihuela and guitar, Victoria wrote only sacred music. On the webite is an early motet, *O magnum mysterium* `website 36`; Victoria later wrote a parody Mass using this motet as the point of departure.

Renaissance Polyphony and the Church

Giovanni Pierluigi (c. 1525/26–1594) was born near Rome in a town called Palestrina and he is always referred to by the name of his birthplace. Organist and choirmaster at his local cathedral by the age of eighteen, he transferred to Rome when the local bishop became Bishop of Rome as Pope Julian III.

Tomás Luis de Victoria (1548–1611)

During Palestrina's lifetime the Catholic Church finally called a council, something that reformers had been repeatedly demanding during several discontented centuries. It was all too late as far as the Protestants were concerned, but the Council of Trent met in a small north Italian town from 1545 to 1563 to tackle the issue of reform in the Church and the response to the Protestant Reformation. Among the many perceived abuses, there were complaints that church music was now corrupted. Choristers lacked reverence, Masses used secular music, the sacred words of the text could not be understood. In 1562, the reforming council decreed that the purpose of singing in church was 'not to give empty pleasure to the ear' but to communicate the Christian message; therefore the words had to be clearly sung and understood by the congregation. Some of the cardinals argued for a complete ban on polyphony, which they saw as the main obstacle to understanding; but the council stopped short of this.

From this comes the appealing legend that Palestrina wrote the *Missa Papae Marcelli* (the 'Mass of Pope Marcellus') website 37 in order to demonstrate that sacred music could be polyphonic and the text still understood. Officially, Palestrina also studiously avoided any pre-existing secular material, and this is therefore the very opposite of a parody Mass. However, some scholars have argued that traces of – of all things – that most popular basis for a parody Mass, *L'homme armé*, are tucked away in it. Might this be a secret act of subversion by a composer who resented being given orders by a totalitarian cultural regime? Different critics have read this in different ways, but

Giovanni Pierluigi da Palestrina
(c. 1525/26–1594)

we should remember that it is only a suggestion. It might equally be the inadvertent result of the composer being too much the child of his time to be able to avoid such influences. It could even be that scholars are trying too hard to find something that isn't there.

However, the tale of Palestrina and the rescuing of polyphony is a story that caught the imagination of the late-Romantic composer Hans Pfitzner, who wrote an opera on the subject. As you listen to sacred Renaissance counterpoint, notice the way that underlying this newly complex music is the plainchant that has been there for so many centuries: much has been added to the music, but nothing has been taken away.

We should not assume that everyone took readily to the new music. Indeed, in concluding, let us turn to a story about a performance of some of Lassus's motets in the streets during a Corpus Christi procession in sixteenth-century Munich. The townspeople, who had not heard such avant-garde music before, thought that the mystifying polyphony was evidence that the court singers were all possessed by the Devil! This may indicate that what was played and found acceptable in educated and advanced court circles was rather different from what was being sung in the street and tavern. So it may have been that gaps were opening up in society which had not been there in the earlier Middle Ages, when costume and performance culture were largely held in common by rich and poor. Perhaps in this, at last, we have tracked down the real divide between the Middle Ages and the Renaissance. Here, certainly, is a cultural division that has persisted to the present day.

Sources of Featured Panels

Page 17: Comnena, Anna, Preface to *The Alexiad*, Penguin Classics, 1969

Page 19: Hill, Rosalind, ed. and trans., *Gesta Francorum et Aliorum Hierosolimitanorum: The Deeds of the Franks and other Pilgrims to Jerusalem*, Clarendon Press, 1967

Page 24: Ladurie, Emmanuel Le Roy, *Montaillou: Cathars and Catholics in a French Village 1294–1324*, Penguin Books 1990

Page 47: Machiavelli, Niccolò, *The Prince*, Penguin Classics, 2003

Page 50: Castillo, Bernal Diaz del, *The Conquest of New Spain*, Penguin Classics, 1969

Page 63: Brett, Philip ed., *The Byrd Edition, Volume 5: Gradualia, Volume 1*, Stainer & Bell, 1989

Pages 66–7: Roper, William, *The Lyfe of Sir Thomas Moore, knighte*, Early English Text Society, 1935

Page 69: Weston, William, ed. and trans. Philip Caraman, *An Autobiography from the Jesuit Underground*, Farrar, Straus and Cudahy, 1955

A Timeline of Early Music

	Music	History
500	c. 500 Boethius *De institutione musica*, the standard source for ancient theory	529 St Benedict founds order of monks
600	c. 650? Roman *schola cantorum* founded	622 prophet Muhammad migrates from Mecca to Medina: Muslim era begins
700	c. 756 Byzantine Emperor sends an organ to Frankish king Pepin III	711 Moors begin conquest of Spain
800	c. 800 earliest surviving books with complete texts of Mass chants	800 Pope crowns Charlemagne Holy Roman Emperor c. 860 conversion of southern Slavs to Christianity
900	c. 900 earliest surviving chant books using neumes to notate pitch c. 994 organ installed at Old Minster, Winchester	c. 965 Denmark and Poland adopt Christianity

Art and Architecture	Literature

532 Hagia Sophia, Constantinople,
begun by Justinian
540 San Vitale, Ravenna, begun

c. 625 Muhammad begins dictating
the Qur'an

c. 700 Lindisfarne Gospels

731 Bede *Ecclesiastical History of the English People*
786 Caliph of Baghdad orders Arabic translations of ancient Greek treatises

c. 800 Book of Kells

c. 892 Alfred the Great translates into Anglo-Saxon works by Boethius and St Augustine

Music	History
1000 c. 1000 Winchester Troper, the earliest surviving collection of church polyphony c. 1020 Guido of Arezzo defines the musical staff 1098 Hildegard of Bingen born	1054 Pope Leo IX excommunicates the Eastern Patriarch: final schism between eastern and western churches 1066 William of Normandy invades England, defeats Harold at Hastings 1076 Emperor Henry IV and German clergy defy Pope Gregory VII over the right to create bishops 1084 Emperor's army occupies Rome and replaces Pope; foundation of Carthusian order 1086–7 English *Domesday Book* 1095 Pope Urban II proclaims First Crusade 1098 foundation of Cistercian order of monks
1100 c. 1150–1250 age of the troubadours and *trouvères* c. 1160–80 Léonin compiles *Magnus liber* (Notre Dame, Paris) 1179 Hildegard of Bingen dies ?c. 1180–90 Pérotin revises *Magnus liber*	1149 Second Crusade preached by St Bernard, abbot of Clairvaux 1154 Henry of Anjou, ruler of extensive lands in France, also becomes King Henry II of England 1158 University of Bologna founded c. 1160–1213 rise of city-states in northern Italy 1189 Third Crusade
1200 c. 1230 *Carmina Burana* compiled c. 1280 Franco of Cologne describes mensural notation, with notes given fixed rhythmic values	1200–30 universities founded at Paris, Oxford, Salamanca, Padua, Cambridge 1209 Albigensian Crusade against heretical Cathars in southern France 1210 Franciscan order founded 1216 Dominican order founded 1248 Ferdinand takes Seville from Moors 1249 Moors driven from Portugal

Art and Architecture	Literature
1042–85 St Mark's, Venice 1063–1118 Pisa cathedral 1075–1188 Santiago de Compostela, Spain 1089–1206 La Madeleine, Vézelay	1050–1100 *The Song of Roland*
1110–33 Durham cathedral nave 1110–81 Worms cathedral 1140 east end at St Denis marks beginning of Gothic style 1153–1278 baptistery of Pisa cathedral 1163–1250 Notre Dame cathedral, Paris 1174 Gothic architecture introduced to England in choir of Canterbury cathedral 1194 Chartres cathedral destroyed by fire, and work begins to rebuild in Gothic style	c. 1150 *Poema del Cid*, Spanish epic c. 1150–1200 Norman mystery play *Mystère d'Adam* 1170 Chrétien de Troyes *Lancelot*
1202–20 Rouen, Reims, Cambrai, Tours, Amiens cathedrals begun 1220–66 Salisbury cathedral ('Early English') 1226 Siena cathedral begun 1228–53 S. Francesco, Assisi 1243–8 Sainte-Chapelle, Paris 1245–69 transepts and nave, Westminster Abbey ('Early English') 1266 Giotto born	c. 1200 German epic *Nibelungenlied* c. 1210 Gottfried von Strassburg *Tristan und Isolde* c. 1225 Guillaume de Lorris *Roman de la Rose* c. 1230 commentaries of Averroes on Aristotle introduced to Europe c. 1250–1300 earliest surviving English mystery play *The Harrowing of Hell*

Music	History
1200 (cont.)	

	Music	History
1300	c. 1325 Francesco Landini born 1325 Pope John XXII cautions against elaborate church polyphony 1340 Machaut made a canon at Reims c. 1370 Machaut *Messe de Notre Dame* 1377 Machaut dies 1397 Landini dies	1309–77 French popes make Avignon their seat c. 1340 height of Moorish civilisation in Granada, Spain 1345 Turks begin to move into Europe 1348–9 Black Death in Europe kills an estimated one-third of the population 1378 beginning of Great Schism in western Church: rival popes in Rome and Avignon 1390 Turks complete conquest of Asia Minor 1391 first siege by Turks of Constantinople
1400	1400 Dufay born ?c. 1415–20 Squarcialupi Codex, a richly illuminated Florentine MS including 352 works c. 1420 Old Hall MS, a large collection of English church music; Dufay in papal choir, Rome 1452 Conrad Paumann *Fundamentum organisandi* 1453 Dunstable dies; Ockeghem working at court of France c. 1460 Josquin des Prez born 1460 Binchois dies 1460–70 *Buxheimer Orgelbuch* compiled 1467 Busnois joins Duke of Burgundy's chapel at Dijon 1474 Dufay dies c. 1485 Josquin serving Sforza family in Milan	1414–17 Council of Constance ends Great Schism 1415 Bohemian reformer John Hus burnt at the stake; English king Henry V revives claim to French throne 1420–60 Prince Henry the Navigator of Portugal encourages exploration of African coastline and Atlantic islands 1431 Joan of Arc burnt at Rouen; Henry VI of England crowned king of France 1434 Cosimo de' Medici establishes ruling dynasty in Florence 1453 Turks take Constantinople; end of Hundred Years War between England and France c. 1455 Johann Gutenberg prints Mazarin Bible using movable type 1474 William Caxton prints books in English

Art and Architecture	Literature
1291 nave, York Minster ('Decorated')	c. 1260 *Njál's Saga* (Icelandic)
1296 Florence cathedral begun	c. 1290–1304 Dante *La vita nuova*
	1298 Marco Polo *Book of Travels*
c. 1305 Giotto paints frescoes in Padua	c. 1307–21 Dante *The Divine*
1322 octagon begun, Ely cathedral	*Comedy*
1334 Palace of the Popes begun,	c. 1350–52 Boccaccio *Decameron*
Avignon	1366 Petrarch *Canzoniere*
1337 Giotto dies	c. 1367 William Langland *Piers*
1385–1485 Milan cathedral	*Plowman*
1386 Donatello born	c. 1380 Bible translated into English
	by Wyclif and others
	1387–1400 Chaucer *Canterbury Tales*
c. 1400 Fra Angelico born	c. 1400 Froissart *Chronicles*
1401 Seville cathedral begun	1425 Thomas à Kempis *De imitatione*
c. 1417 *Très Riches Heures* of the Duc	*Christi*
de Berry	1463–9 Marsilio Ficino translates
c. 1420 Brunelleschi begins work on	dialogues of Plato into Latin
dome of Florence cathedral (to 1436)	c. 1467 Erasmus born
1432 Jan van Eyck finishes painting	1470 Sir Thomas Malory completes
Adoration of the Lamb for Ghent	*Le morte d'Arthur*
cathedral	1474 Ludovico Ariosto born
1435 Leone Battista Alberti's book *De*	1480 Angelo Poliziano *Favola di*
pictura explains rules of perspective	*Orfeo*
c. 1435 Fra Angelico *Coronation of the*	c. 1494 Rabelais born
Virgin	
?c. 1440 Donatello *David*	
1444 Botticelli born	
1446 King's College Chapel, Cambridge	
begun ('Perpendicular')	
c. 1450 Hieronymus Bosch born	
1452 Leonardo born; Ghiberti's bronze	
doors completed, Florence baptistery	

Music	History
1400 1490 Josquin in papal chapel at (cont.) Rome 1490–1502 *Eton Choirbook* 1495 Tinctoris *Terminorum musicae diffinitorium* (first printed dictionary of music) 1497 Ockeghem dies	1478 Ferdinand of Aragon and Isabella of Castile together establish Inquisition against heresy in Spain 1492 Columbus reaches Bahamas; final defeat of Moors in Spain by Ferdinand and Isabella 1494 Charles VIII of France invades Italy to claim throne of Naples; Medici expelled from Florence; treaty of Tordesillas divides New World between Spain and Portugal 1498 Savonarola dies in Florence
1500 1501 Petrucci, in Venice, prints the first music books from movable type c. 1505 Tallis born 1505 Obrecht dies 1517 Isaac dies 1521 Josquin dies 1525 Palestrina born 1527 Attaingnant prints his first collection of *chansons* in Paris; Willaert appointed *maestro di cappella* of St Mark's, Venice 1538 Willaert First Book of Madrigals 1542 *Geneva Psalter* 1543 Byrd born; Susato begins publishing (Antwerp) 1551 Palestrina at Cappella Giulia, Rome 1554 Palestrina First Book of Masses 1555 Palestrina at St John Lateran, Rome 1556 Lassus at court of Albrecht V, Munich; Lassus First Book of Motets	1500 France and Spain agree to divide kingdom of Naples 1505 France cedes Naples to Spain 1512 Spanish restore Medici to Florence 1517 Luther nails his ninety-five theses to door of castle church at Wittenberg 1519–21 Spanish under Cortés conquer Aztecs in Mexico; Ferdinand Magellan makes first circumnavigation of the world 1520 Luther publishes three Reformation treatises, and publicly burns papal bull of excommunication 1524 Peasants' Revolt in Germany 1527 Rome sacked by Spanish and German troops, Pope Clement VII captured; Sweden adopts Lutheranism 1529 Turks besiege Vienna

Art and Architecture	Literature
1458 Palazzo Pitti begun, Florence	
1465 Giovanni Bellini *The Agony in the Garden*	
1466 Donatello dies	
1471 Dürer born	
1473–81 Sistine Chapel, Rome, built and partially decorated	
1475 Michelangelo born	
c. 1480 Botticelli *La primavera*; Bosch *The Crucifixion*	
1481–1537 St George's Chapel, Windsor ('Perpendicular')	
1483 Raphael born; Leonardo moves to Milan, receives commission to paint *Virgin of the Rocks* altarpiece	
c. 1485 Titian born	
c. 1495–97 Leonardo *The Last Supper*	

Art and Architecture	Literature
1500 Dürer *Self-Portrait*	c. 1500 English morality play *Everyman*
c. 1500–06 Leonardo *Mona Lisa*	
1501–04 Michelangelo *David*	c. 1514 Machiavelli *The Prince*
1506 Bramante's St Peter's begun, Rome	1516 Ariosto *Orlando Furioso*; Thomas More *Utopia*
1508–12 Michelangelo ceiling of Sistine Chapel, Rome; Raphael working on frescoes of Vatican apartments, inc. *School of Athens*	1524 Ronsard born
	1528 Baldassare Castiglione *The Book of the Courtier*
1510 Botticelli dies; Giorgione dies	1533 Montaigne born
1513 Dürer *Knight, Death and the Devil*	1534 François Rabelais *Gargantua*
1516 Bosch dies	1536 Erasmus dies
1516–18 Titian *Assumption of the Virgin*	1550 Ronsard first four books of *Odes*
1519 Leonardo dies	1561 Hoby *The Courtyer* (English translation of Castiglione)
1520 Raphael dies	
c. 1525–30 Bruegel born	1564 Shakespeare born
1528 Dürer dies; Grünewald dies	1573 Torquato Tasso *Aminta*
1533 Holbein *The Ambassadors*	1577 Holinshed *Chronicles*
1536 Michelangelo begins *The Last Judgement*	1581 Tasso *Gerusalemme liberata*
1550 Vasari *Lives of the Artists*	1587 Christopher Marlowe *Tamburlaine the Great*
1553 Titian *Danaë*	
1563 El Escorial begun, near Madrid	1590 Edmund Spenser *The Faerie Queene*
1564 Michelangelo dies	c. 1591 Shakespeare *Richard III*

Music	History
1500 (cont.)	1558 Zarlino *Le istitutioni harmoniche*	1533 Henry VIII of England excommunicated for divorcing his queen to marry Anne Boleyn

1558 Zarlino *Le istitutioni harmoniche*	1533 Henry VIII of England excommunicated for divorcing his queen to marry Anne Boleyn
1563 Byrd at Lincoln Cathedral	1534 Henry VIII becomes supreme head of the English Church; Society of Jesus founded in Spain by Ignatius Loyola
1565 Zarlino at St Mark's, Venice	
1567 Monteverdi born	
1569 Victoria in Rome	
1570 Byrd at Chapel Royal, London	1541 Calvin sets up Puritan theocracy in Geneva; Turks conquer Hungary
1577 Sweelinck at Oude Kerk, Amsterdam	
1580 Marenzio First Book of Madrigals	1543 Copernicus *De revolutionibus orbium coelestium* rejects traditional view of earth as the centre of the universe
1582 Monteverdi's first publication	
1586 Giovanni Gabrieli organist at St Mark's, Venice	
1587 Victoria in Madrid	1545 Council of Trent convened in reply to threat of the Reformation
1588 Byrd, *Psalms, sonets and songs*	1555 Holy Roman Empire grants freedom of worship to Lutheran states in Germany
1589 grandest of all sets of *intermedi* (for a Medici wedding, Florence)	
	1562 start of religious wars in France between Huguenots and Catholics
1591 Monteverdi in Mantua	1567 Philip II of Spain imposes reign of terror on the Netherlands following Protestant uprising
1597 G. Gabrieli *Sacrae symphoniae*; Dowland First Book of Songs; Morley *A Plaine and Easie Introduction to Practicall Musicke*	
	1571 Battle of Lepanto, where Spanish and Venetian fleets defeat Turks
1598 Peri *Dafne*, Florence (the first opera)	1572 Massacre of St Bartholomew, Paris (over 20,000 Huguenots killed)
	1579–81 Northern provinces of Netherlands set up Dutch Republic and break away from Spain
	1588 Spanish naval supremacy ends with defeat of the Armada
	1593–1606 Austria at war with Turks
	1598 Philip II of Spain dies; edict of Nantes in France grants Huguenots equal rights with Catholics

Art and Architecture	Literature
1565 Bruegel *The Months*	1592 Montaigne dies
1571 Caravaggio born	c. 1595 Shakespeare *Romeo and Juliet*
1575 Titian dies	1597 Bacon *Essays*
1577 Rubens born	1598 Ben Jonson *Every Man in His Humour*
1586–88 El Greco *Burial of Count Orgaz*	
1599 van Dyck born; Velásquez born; Caravaggio given contract for paintings in San Luigi dei Francesi, Rome	

Early Music Composers

Agricola, Alexander (c. 1445/46–1506)
(*b.* Ghent, S. Netherlands; *d.* Valladolid, Spain)

Arcadelt, Jacques (?1507–1568)
(*b.* ?nr Namur, S. Netherlands; *d.* France)

Binchois, Gilles (c. 1400–1460)
(*b.* ?Mons, S. Netherlands; *d.* Soignies, S. Netherlands)

Bourgeois, Louis (c. 1510/15–1559)
(*b.* Paris, France; *d.* Paris, France)

Busnois, Antoine (c. 1430–1492)
(*b.* Busnes, Artois, France; *d.* Burgundy, France)

Byrd, William (c. 1540–1623)
(*b.* London, England; *d.* Stondon Massey, England)

Dowland, John (1563–1626)
(*b.* ?London, England; *d.* London, England)

Dufay, Guillaume (1397–1474)
(*b.* Beersel, S. Netherlands; *d.* Cambrai, France)

Dunstable, John (c. 1385–1453)
(*b.* England; *d.* England)

Gesualdo, Carlo (c. 1561–1613)
(*b.* ?Naples, Italy; *d.* Gesualdo, Italy)

Gibbons, Orlando (1583–1625)
(*b.* Oxford, England; *d.* Canterbury, England)

Gombert, **Nicolas** (c. 1495–c. 1556)
(*b.* ?La Gorgue, S. Netherlands; *d.* ?Tournai, S. Netherlands)

Goudimel, **Claude** (c. 1514/20–1572)
(*b.* Besançon, France; *d.* Lyons, France)

Guido of Arezzo (c. 991/92–after 1033)
(*b.* Italy; *d.* Italy)

Henry VIII (1491–1547)
(*b.* Greenwich, England; *d.* Windsor, England)

Hildegard of Bingen (1098–1179)
(*b.* Bermersheim, nr Alzey, Germany; *d.* Rupertsberg, nr Bingen, Germany)

Isaac [Issac], **Heinrich** (c. 1450/55–1517)
(*b.* Flanders or Brabant, S. Netherlands; *d.* Florence, Italy)

Janequin, **Clément** (c. 1485–after 1558)
(*b.* Châtellerault, France; *d.* Paris, France)

Landini, **Francesco** (c. 1325–1397)
(*b.* ?Fiesole or Florence, Italy; *d.* Florence, Italy)

Lassus, **Orlande de** (c. 1532–1594)
(*b.* Mons, S. Netherlands; *d.* Munich, Germany)

Léonin (*fl.* Paris, France, 1150s–c. 1201)

Machaut, **Guillaume de** (c. 1300–1377)
(*b.* Reims or Machault, France; *d.* Reims, France)

Morton, **Robert** (1430–after 1479)
(*b.* England; *d.* ?England)

Mudarra, **Alonso** (c. 1510–1580)
(*b.* Spain; *d.* Seville, Spain)

Obrecht, **Jacob** (1457/8–1505)
(*b.* Ghent, S. Netherlands; *d.* Ferrara, Italy)

Ockeghem, **Johannes** (c. 1410–1497)
(*b.* Saint-Ghislain, nr Mons, S. Netherlands; *d.* ?Tours, France)

Palestrina, Giovanni Pierluigi da (c. 1525/26–1594)
(*b.* ?Palestrina, Italy; *d.* Rome, Italy)

Pérotin (*fl.* Paris, France, c. 1200)

Prez, Josquin des (c. 1450/55–c. 1521)
(*b.* ?nr Saint-Quentin, France; *d.* Condé-sur-l'Escaut, France)

Riquier, Guiraut (c. 1230–c. 1300)
(*b.* Narbonne, France; *d.* ?)

Rudel, Jaufre (*fl.* 1120–47)

Sachs, Hans (1494–1576)
(*b.* Nuremberg, Germany; *d.* Nuremberg, Germany)

Sheppard, John (c. 1515–1558)
(*b.* England; *d.* England)

Striggio, Alessandro c. 1536/37–1592)
(*b.* Mantua, Italy; *d.* Mantua, Italy)

Susato, Tylman (c. 1510/15–1570 or later)
(*b.* Soest, S. Netherlands; *d.* ?Sweden)

Tallis, Thomas (c. 1505–1585)
(*b.* England; *d.* Greenwich, England)

Taverner, John (c. 1490–1545)
(*b.* South Lincs., England; *d.* Boston, Lincs., England)

Tye, Christopher (c. 1505–?1573)
(*b.* England; *d.* England)

Victoria, Tomás Luis de (1548–1611)
(*b.* Avila, Spain; *d.* Madrid, Spain)

Vitry, Philippe de (1291–1361)
(*b.* ?Champagne, France; *d.* France)

Willaert, Adrian (c. 1490–1562)
(*b.* Bruges or Roulaers, S. Netherlands; *d.* Venice, Italy)

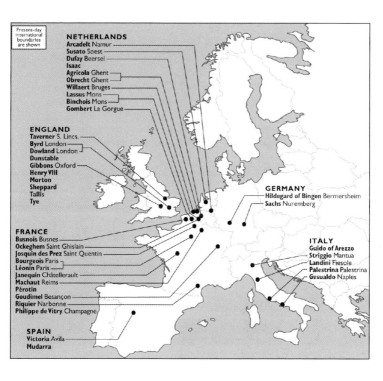

Map showing birthplaces of early music composers

Glossary

Albigensian	person or idea associated with the French town of Albi; specifically Catharist person or idea (see also Catharism)
Ars antiqua	Latin for 'old art', a term coined by French theorists in the fourteenth century to describe the music of the twelfth and thirteenth centuries (see also *Ars nova*)
Ars nova	Latin for 'new art', first used in a treatise written by Philippe de Vitry in around 1322 (see also *Ars antiqua*)
Ballade	a medieval French song with a regular poetic and musical structure; an example of a *forme fixe*
Bard	Celtic poet–musician
Caccia	type of Medieval Italian song, originally describing hunting, but later also tackling other secular topics, notably courtship
Cantiga	form of medieval Spanish monophonic song
Cantus firmus	pre-existing melody adopted as the basis of a piece of polyphonic music
Carol	a song that celebrates religious or secular events or themes, usually consisting of several verses and a repeating chorus
Catharism	medieval heresy in which believers were taught that the physical world was evil and that the spirit needed to be freed from it

Chromaticism the inclusion of notes from outside the scale of the key in which the music is written. Music is normally written in such a way as to be in a recognisable key (for example, C major) or mode (for example, Dorian). Each key or mode has a sequence of notes that makes up a scale (for example, the 'C major scale'). When composers add notes from outside the scale, it adds to the richness and emotional complexity of the music.

Consort an ensemble of instruments. A whole consort is one where all the players use instruments belonging to the same family, e.g., all recorders or all viols. A broken consort is a group which includes members of different instrument families, e.g., a group of viols with one lute.

Cornemuse bagpipe

Counterpoint polyphonic music in which two or more individual melodic lines are played or sung simultaneously (see also Polyphony)

Crwth the Welsh name for a bowed lyre with a bridge and fingerboard; known as a 'crowd' in English

Discant music in which an extra voice is added to a plainchant line, often moving in contrary motion

Formes fixes types of medieval French song with specified musical and verse structures, such as *ballade*, *rondeau* and *virelai*

Galliard lively Renaissance dance, originating in Italy, in duple time and often performed after the statelier pavan

Gregorian chant liturgical plainchant

Hymn a type of sacred song setting non-biblical text in contrast with a psalm (see also Psalm)

Isorhythm a repeating rhythmic pattern, characteristic of *ars nova* music

Jongleur a versatile medieval entertainer of lowly status, who could usually sing, dance and tell jokes (see also Minstrel)

Lauda spirituale a type of sacred song usually setting a non-biblical Italian text (see also *Cantiga* and Carol)

Ludus Latin for 'game' or 'play'

Lute a pear-shaped plucked-string instrument made of wood. It is played broadly like a guitar and achieved its greatest popularity in the Renaissance.

Madrigal initially, a medieval Italian song with a regular poetic (rhyming) and musical structure; cited as an example of Italian *ars nova* by those who use the term when discussing Italian late medieval music. Subsequently, the word was revived to describe the most successful song form in Renaissance Europe.

Mass Christian religious service taking its name from the Latin ('missa') which includes the Eucharist, a ritual commemoration of the Last Supper (see also Ordinary and Proper)

Melisma a group of notes sung to a single syllable of text. Plainchant is originally one syllable per note, but melismatic passages became standard practice from early on in the history of church music.

Minnesinger medieval German poet–musician, influenced by troubadours and *trouvères*, particularly notable for writing love songs

Minstrel all-purpose word for medieval entertainer, especially a singer. Minstrels were generally musically and textually illiterate, and performed their large repertoire from memory. They were sometimes attached to a specific family and sometimes itinerant (see also Jongleur).

Mode one of a series of musical scales that were defined as part of the standardisation of plainchant. The scales were given Greek names adopted from Byzantine practice and were believed to derive from classical Greek music, though the connection with the latter may have been either non-existent or coincidental. Medieval musical theory expected specific modes to be both expressive and stimulating of specific emotions, though there was little agreement about which mode was associated with which emotion.

Monophony music consisting of a single melodic line with no accompaniment

Neume a written sign in medieval notation, an early way of writing down music. A neumatic style is likely to consist of one note per syllable.

Ordinary parts of the Mass the texts of which do not vary, i.e., Kyrie, Gloria, Credo, Sanctus, Benedictus and Agnus Dei

Ordo Latin for 'play' or 'drama'

Organum medieval polyphony in which one or more parts are sung at the same time as a (different) plainchant melody

Parody Mass A musical setting of the five movements of the Ordinary of the Roman Catholic Mass based on the imitative texture of a pre-existing polyphonic composition

Pavan a stately Renaissance dance involving a sequence of two steps and then a double step like a leap or hop. Pavans were often paired with a contrastingly livelier dance, such as the saltarello in Italy or the galliard in England.

Plainsong an alternative name for plainchant

Plainchant monophonic medieval religious music, including Ambrosian chant and Gregorian chant

Polyphony music using more than one melodic line sounding simultaneously

Polytextual music in which more than one text or set of words is sung simultaneously

Proper   parts of the Mass the texts of which vary with the day and season, i.e., Introit, Gradual, Alleluia, Track, Offertory and Communion

Psalm   a religious song the text of which is taken from the Book of Psalms in the Old Testament

Psalter   a book containing psalms for use in church services

Responsory   medieval liturgical plainchant in which different voices or groups of voices sing in turn; later set in polyphonic form by Renaissance composers

Rondeau   a medieval French song with a regular poetic (rhyming) and musical structure; an example of a *forme fixe*

Scop   Anglo-Saxon poet

Sequence   liturgical plainchant hymn

Talea   isorhythmic unit

Trope   text added to a melisma, notably to the *Jubilus* of an Alleluia

Troubadour   medieval poet–musician in southern France, writing in Occitan (Provençal)

Trouvère   medieval north-French troubadour

Vihuela   member of the viol family of instruments but played like a guitar

Viol   a bowed string instrument that originated in Spain. It has an arched bridge and is held and played on the lap or between the knees depending on its size. Often described as the ancestor of the cello, the playing posture is similar, but viols generally possess six strings in contrast to the standard four of the violin family. Viols were made in several different sizes and a complete set was known in English as a 'chest', as that was where they were stored. A viol ensemble was called a consort, and such groups remained popular with composers and audiences in England, even after they had gone out of fashion in Italy and France.

Virelai   a medieval French song with a regular poetic (rhyming) and musical structure; an example of a *forme fixe*

About the Author

Lucien Jenkins is the founder of *Early Music Today*, *Classroom Music* and *Teaching Drama*, and former editor of *Music Teacher*. He is the author of *Laying out the Body* (poems from Seren Books), *Romanticism in Focus* and *Modernism in Focus* (Rhinegold), and co-author of the *Classical Music Encyclopedia* (Collins). His editions of *The Necromancer* by Peter Teuthold and *The Midnight Bell* by Francis Lathom (two of the Gothic novels cited in Austen's *Northanger Abbey)* were welcomed by *The Year's Work in English Studies*.

He studied for his BA at Cambridge University, and for his MA and PhD at London University. He has taught for Ruskin College, Oxford, the Open University and Bristol University's lifelong learning department, and has worked as a reviewer, critic and journalist for history, literature, dance, music and the visual arts.

Index